Rabbi Nachm

RESTORE MY SOUL!

Meshivat Nefesh

Translated by: Avraham Greenbaum
with an introduction by
Rabbi Aryeh Kaplan

ISBN 0-930213-13-0

for further information:
Breslov Research Institute
PO Box 5370
Jerusalem, Israel
or:
Breslov Research Institute
POB 587
Monsey, NY 10952-0587
USA
or:
Breslov Charitable Foundation
33, Waterpark Road
Salford, M7 0FT
Manchester, England

With praise and thanks to HaShem

on the occasion

of the wedding of our children,

Elisha Nachman and Shoshanna Malka

* * *

May the merit of

Rebbe Nachman ben Faige

continue to be a blessing

for all of us and *Klal* Yisrael

The Family of **R' Tzvi Yehuda Levinson**

PUBLISHER'S PREFACE

Torat Hashem temima, MESHIVAT NAFESH, eidut Hashem ne'emana, machkimat peti. "The Torah of the Lord is perfect, RESTORING THE SOUL, the testimony of the Lord is sure, making wise the simple" (Psalms 19:8).

The *Yalkut Shimoni* in a comment on this passage asks: "Why is the Torah perfect? Because it RESTORES THE SOUL. How can the Torah RESTORE THE SOUL? Because it is perfect. When can the Torah restore the soul? When it comes from one who is perfect. When is the testimony sure? When it comes from one who is trustworthy" (*Yal. Shim.* Ps. 19, Par. 674)

Rabbi Alter of Teplik was one of the leading Breslover Chassidim in Europe at the turn of the century. He foresaw the spiritual holocaust that was descending upon the Jewish people. Inspired by Rabbi Nachman's cry, *"Gevalt!* Never give up *hope!"* R. Alter collected from Rabbi Nachman's book *Lekutey Moharan* and from that of his disciple, R. Nathan, *Lekutey Halachot,* all the sections dealing with inner fortitude and optimism. A clear message emerges. Man should know that he can always return to God, regardless of the condition he may be in. R. Alter called the book *Meshivat Nefesh.*

Rabbi Nachman explains (Lek. Moh. B#7) that there is a concept of *ayeh?* and a concept of *maleh.* The concept of *ayeh?* is derived from the cry of the angels, *"Where* is the place of His glory?" There are people who have advanced to high levels in the service of God. Even so, they must still ask "Where?" They have to be shown that they still have far to go to reach God.

The concept of *maleh* is derived from the praise of the angels, "The whole earth is *filled* with His glory"(Is. 6:3). There is no place that is devoid of the glory of God. People on the lowest levels should know that God is right next to them. With this understanding they can strengthen themselves to return to God.

The Zohar (I, 31a) states "The Tzadik joins the heavens and the earth." Only a person who has attained such a lofty position can unify the earth — that is, the people who are on the earth — with the heavens, that is, God. This is the meaning of the comment of the *Yalkut:* "When can the Torah restore the soul? When it comes from one who is perfect. When is the testimony sure? When it comes from one who is trustworthy." The Tzadik is the one who is perfect and trustworthy.

The text of this translation of *Meshivat Nefesh* is accompanied by notes which are intended to serve as a guide to the sources of the many quotations from the Bible, the Talmud, the Midrash and the kabbalistic writings. There are also notes aimed at clarifying certain ideas found in the text. This edition of *Meshivat Nefesh* includes all the passages in the original edition which were drawn from the writings of Rabbi Nachman himself. Only a selection of the passages drawn from the writings of Rabbi Nathan has been included owing to reasons of space. The paragraphing of the original Hebrew text has been followed. Where a passage has been omitted, the original paragraph number is printed in parentheses to indicate where it may be found for those who wish to refer to the original.

Yeshivat Breslov would like to express its sincere thanks to Avraham Greenbaum for his efforts in translating this truly remarkable work. Avraham Greenbaum has written about Rabbi Nachman and his teachings for Britain's Jewish press. A radio producer with the British Broadcasting Corporation, Avraham Greenbaum produced a full length feature programme on Rabbi Nachman's life and teachings which was broadcast on BBC Radio 4 in April 1980.

Our thanks are due to Rabbi Aryeh Kaplan for his advice in the planning of this book and for his introduction.

May it be the will of the Almighty that through the restoration of our souls we shall merit the coming of the Messiah and the restoration of the Holy Temple, and that (Is. 52:8) "Eye to eye we shall see the return of the *Shechina* to Tziyon and Jerusalem." Amen.

Chaim Kramer

INTRODUCTION

by Rabbi Aryeh Kaplan

It is very easy to live when things go right. But what about when things go wrong? What does one do then? What does one do when everything in the world seems to go against him?

From time immemorial, our sages have taught us that if a person trusts in God, he has every reason to be optimistic. While troubles may come, they are always temporary -- nothing lasts forever. Thus, there is the famous legend that King Solomon, the wisest man of all time, had a ring inscribed with the words, "This too will pass."

Even the most successful people have gone through difficult times. Indeed, it is sometimes the very difficulties that they have experienced that gives them the steel to become successful. No better example of this is the author, Rabbi Nachman himself, who overcame many difficulties in his youth to become one of the greatest leaders of modern times.

The idea is perhaps best expressed in a story told by Rabbi Nachman:

There was once a man who earned his living by digging clay. Once he happened to find a particularly valuable diamond in his diggings. Knowing that the only place where he could find a proper market for the stone was in London, he decided to travel there. He did not have any money however, and when

he took a ship, he showed the captain the diamond and told him that he would be amply rewarded when they reached their destination.

The captain was impressed with the man, and gave him the best first class cabin. The man was in the habit of placing the stone on the table while he ate, since just looking at it would put him in a good mood. One day, after a particularly sumptuous meal, he fell asleep, leaving the diamond on the table. When the steward cleaned off the table, he shook everything on the tablecloth off into the sea,--including the diamond.

When the man woke up, he immediately realized what had happened. But what to do? If he would tell the captain, he would immediately lose all his status--and who knows what the captain might do. So he made believe that nothing had happened, and maintained a spirit of optimism, both inwardly and outwardly.

Meanwhile, the captain had a problem. He had a cargo of wheat designated for England, but he learned that if he would deliver it in his own name, he could have severe legal difficulties. Confiding in the man, he asked him to do him a favor, and sign a bill of lading placing all the wheat in his (the man's) name. Feeling that this would give him some security upon their arrival, he quickly agreed.

The ship continued its journey. Then, shortly before it arrived in England, the captain suddenly died. There was the young man with an entire shipload of wheat in his name. It was worth far more than his diamond, and the man would now be very wealthy. It was all the result of his optimism.

Rabbi Nachman concluded this story by saying, "The diamond did not belong to the man; the proof is, that it did not remain with him. The wheat was meant to be his; the proof is that it did remain with him. He had his good fortune only because he did not let his misfortune overwhelm him."

"He did not let his misfortune overwhelm him!" If anything, this is the lesson of this book--and one of the important teachings of Rabbi Nachman. No matter how bad things may be, God can always make them become better.

"But," you may ask, "what about a person suffering and dying with terminal cancer?" "What about the person who really has no hope?"

But the truth is, that if a person really believes in God and His goodness, he knows that even death itself is not a cause for despair. Just as God watches over a person during life, so will He watch over him after death. The one who truly believes knows that death is more of a beginning than an end. And so, even the terminal cancer victim has hope in a future, bright beyond imagination.

Thus, it is told that when Rabbi Nachman was dying of tuberculosis (which was incurable in his time), he once told his daughter, that he looks at death as nothing more traumatic than walking from one room into another. His disciples say that at the time of his death, there was an unbelievable aura of calmness and serenity about him--as if he were anticipating a beautific experience.

A great-grandson of the Baal Shem Tov, Rabbi Nachman was active in the Ukraine between approximately 1790 and

1810. Although it was an extremely difficult time for Jews, he led his followers with a spirit of unadulterated optimism. Optimism, hope, and trust in God were his watchwords. It is said that in what should have been one of the darkest hours of his life--with his body torn by tuberculosis--one of his most important messages rang forth: *"Gevalt! Never give up hope!"*

This message is every bit as relevant today as it was when first uttered almost 200 years ago.

When asked, "What is in reality the power of choice?" the Rebbe answered "Simple. If you want, you do, if not, not. Too many people are trapped in the customs of their habits, but if they truly want to, they can easily overcome."

A student was once complaining to Rabbi Nachman about his lack of accomplishment in serving God. He said that he wanted very much to serve God. Rabbi Nachman said to him "Do you *truly want* to desire?"

LEKUTEY MOHARAN

1. A person who wishes to return to God must be knowledgeable in God's Law. That is to say, he must have the skill to travel along the path to God.[1] Then nothing in the world will cause him to fall or distance him from God, whether he rises or descends. Regardless of what happens, he should remain strong and follow the guidance of King David: "If I ascend to the Heaven, there You are; and if I make hell my bed, behold You are there." (Ps. 139,8). Even in the lowest pit of hell, a person can draw himself closer to God Almighty, for even there He can be found. This is the meaning of the words of the Psalm: "If I make hell my bed, behold You are there". (*Likutey Moharan* I: 6).

When a person wishes to return to God, he needs two types of skill in the law. He must be skilled in the "running" and skilled in the "returning."[2] These two concepts underlie the

---

1. The Hebrew word for law, *halacha*, is derived from the root "to journey."

2. See Ezekiel 1:14. "The *Chayot* ran and returned as an appearance of a flash of lightning." Man, in his service of G-d also has his times when he "runs (forward) and returns."

words of the Psalm. The skill in the running is necessary at the moment of the "rise up to the Heavens." The skill in returning is required "if I make hell my bed." A person who wants to return to God must gird his loins and strengthen himself in the ways of God at all times. If he climbs higher in his quests, "If I ascend to Heaven," — then — "there You are". And if he experiences a descent — "If I make hell my bed" — he will still find God: "You are there."

This means that if, on the one hand, he is worthy of achieving ascent to a certain level, whether it is great or small, he should not stand still on this level. He should not content himself with it. The skill here is to know and believe that he must advance further and further. This is the idea of the skill in the "running." On the other hand, even if he should fall, God forbid, then regardless of the place to which he has fallen, even if it be the lowest pit of hell, he should never give up hope in any way. Whatever comes upon him, he must search out and entreat God and remain strong in whatever way he can, whatever position he is in. Even in the lowest pit of hell, God is to be found. There, too, a person is able to attach himself to God. For this he must have skill in "returning." "If I make hell my bed, behold You are there."

It is possible to return to God only by acquiring skill in these two ways. It certainly requires great skill and merit to know that at all times we must strive and toil in the service of God. We must yearn at every moment to reach the next higher level. A person must let nothing throw him down, regardless of his condition. He should never come to look down upon himself in any way. When he achieves these two skills, he will be able to travel the path of return to God. The hand of God will be stretched out to receive his repentance. He will be worthy of finding the glory of God and Man will be returned to the throne.[3] Happy is the man who is worthy of this.(*Ibid.*)

2.   The essence of God's greatness is that even those who are farthest of all from Him can still draw near to His service. Through this, God's name is glorified and exalted in the worlds above and the worlds below. It follows from this that nobody should ever despair of drawing close to God's service on account of being far removed from Him because of the many sins he has committed. This is true even if he has committed the gravest wrongs. On the contrary, it is through this person more than anyone, that God's glory is elevated, praised and magnified. In essence, it is through the Tsadikim of the age that those who are far can draw close to God.   (*Ibid.* 10)

3.   Friends who have drawn close to true Tsadikim should try to strengthen one another and give each other encouragement. The strongest support they can give each other is to bear in mind and remind one another of the tremendous spiritual

---

3.   Ezekiel 1:26. *Teshuva* — repentance has its source in *binah* the equivalent of the World of the Throne *(olam habriah)*. When he continues on the path of repentance he is elevated to even higher levels. Hence the reference to the Man who sits on the Throne.

4.   When *Yitro* came to *Moshe Rabenu* in the desert, he said, (Ex. 18:11) "Now I know that God is above all g-ds." *Yitro* was a high priest to idols and after serving them he rejected them and found God. The Zohar (II—69a) states that when *Yitro* spoke, the glory of God rose and was made known is all the heavens and far corners of the earth. Someone like *Yitro*, who was so far from God and now recognizes God from his low level causes the name of the Lord to be revealed in even the lowest levels where he is at.

power of the true Tsadik. This power is so great that it can bring elevation even to the most blemished soul, one which has not yet emerged from the profane to the sacred even by one hair's breadth. The Tsadik has the power to draw up this soul and restore it to good. For even the worst man, regardless of who he might be, and into whatever circumstances he might have sunken at present — so long as he grasps hold of the true Tsadik, there is hope for him to achieve a unique good that will endure forever. Friends should support one another with this knowledge and give each other encouragement. They should strengthen one another in the service of God. Each one should make it his duty to remind his friend of all the teachings they have learned, each one to the full extent of his own understanding.   (*Ibid.* 13)

4. You should know that God derives glory even from the most insignificant of the Children of Israel, even from the sinners of Israel. Every single one — so long as he is called by the name of Israel — gives God a particular glory which no-one else can give. It follows that no one should ever despair of God. Even if he has caused great damage, God forbid, God's love for him has not ceased. This person can still return to God. It is the men of truth who are able to detect the goodness and the glory which are to be found in even the worst of men, and to draw up everything to God.[5]   (*Ibid.* 13)

5. When a man has to rise from one level to the next, prior to his ascent he must first undergo a descent. The paradox is that the very purpose of the descent is the ascent. From this you can see how much strength is required in the service of

5. See preface.

God. Even when you fall or descend in any way, you must never allow yourself to be thrown off balance to the extent that you come to look down upon yourself or to hold yourself in contempt. You should refuse to dwell on the matter even momentarily. Regardless of what happens to you, in the end you will find that all your descents will be turned into great ascents and achievements, because the purpose of the decent is the ascent. This point needs a lot of emphasis because everybody who experiences a spiritual fall imagines that this idea was never intended to refer to his particular case. He thinks it applies only to people on the highest plane who are perpetually climbing from level to level. You should know and have faith that in truth all these words were spoken with even the worst and most insignificant of men in mind, because God is good to all.   (*Ibid* 22)

6.   When a person wishes to enter into the service of God — and this applies to everybody, even one who is on the lowest of levels, even one who is literally "in the earth," he must at all times advance and rise from level to level. Now, every time a person is about to move from one level to the next, each in his own way, he has to encounter the full force of the *kelipot*, the husks, all over again. These are all his desires and fantasies and wild thoughts, the distractions and obstacles which are ranged against a person at every moment and try to prevent him from entering the gates of sanctity.

This often leads to great confusion in the minds of honest people who have truly worked hard on themselves. Suddenly they find all these old desires, confusions and obstacles rising up against them. They start thinking that they must have fallen from their level because before this they had had rest from all these desires and confusions. They lay dormant. Now that they have reappeared, these people come to think they must have fallen down. But this is no fall. What is happening is that the time has come for them to advance from one level to the next, each in his own way. This is why all the desires and confusions and obstacles — all the "crookedness in the heart" — are stirred up against them with fresh force.

Each time this happens you must fortify yourself and refuse to lose heart. Strengthen yourself against these forces and break them anew.   (*Ibid*. 25)

7.   The best thing to do when this happens is to give charity to people who are in genuine need. The true greatness of the Creator is revealed through charity which is given to honest people who are in genuine need. It is through this that the Holy One, blessed be He, is magnified and glorified. Then it becomes possible to crush the *kelipot*, the husks — the obstacles and the confusions — which lurk at each and every level.   (*Ibid*.)

8.   Another way to fight the husks is to bring yourself to joy and delight because of the vital spark which burns within you, the "good point." Think of the true preciousness of being of the seed of Israel, of having drawn close to men of truth who can lead you and guide you along the path of truth. This gives you the hope of gaining enduring good. Through this joy you can break the husks and obstacles which lurk at every level.   (*Ibid*.)

Your friend is also helped when you fortify yourself and break though the obstacles so as to keep on moving up to the next level. A moment ago your friend was standing on the very level which you have now entered. So now your friend also has to move on and rise to an even higher level. It is impossible for two people to stand on one level. A person can actually lift his friend up and bring him up higher. *(Ibid.)*

9. When a person finds that sexual fantasies keep entering his mind, this may be a sign of true repentance. When a person breaks his desires and refuses to pay any attention to them, this is the way he rights the wrongs he did in former times when he abused the Sacred Covenant.[6] True repentance has to balance the wrongs of the past. So a person should not become demoralized if he sees that his head is filled with desires and every kind of corrupt thoughts. In fact he is engaged in the process of righting his own wrongs of the past. For now, instead of succumbing, he stands up against these thoughts and resists them. In this way he achieves true repentance, and he elevates the sparks of holiness which fell through his earlier abuse of the Sacred Covenant.*(Ibid. 27)*

10. "The whole earth is filled with God's glory" (Is. 6:3). There is no place devoid of God. He fills all the worlds and He encompasses all the worlds. Even a person whose occupation is trading with the gentiles cannot excuse himself and say "I cannot serve God" because of the materialism which burdens him through his business. Godliness exists in everything — even in material things and in all the languages of the gentiles.

---

6. Referring to the Covenant of Abraham (Gen. 17). Though the Torah is speaking of the *mitzvoh* of circumcision, it is generally known to include all laws relating to the sanctity of sexual relations, nocturnal pollution etc. The Zohar (I—59b) states, "He who guards his *bris* is known as a Tsadik."

Without Godliness they would have no vitality and they could not endure for a moment. It is only that the lower the level, the more "contracted" is Godliness and the more heavily veiled it is.   *(Ibid. 33)*

11.   Because of this you should know that even if you are sunk in the very domain of the *kelipot*, the husks, and you are on the lowest of levels, at the point where you imagine that it is impossible for you ever to draw close to God because you are so far from him — here still you can find God; you can attach yourself to Him and return in perfect repentance. For "It is not far from you" (Deut. 30:11). It is just that in the place where you are now there are more garments concealing the Godliness.   *(Ibid.)*

12.   There are people who have done so much wrong that they fall to the level of the "concealment within the concealment." Because of this they come to believe that there is no longer any hope for them, God forbid. This is because, when a person does something wrong several times, the matter becomes permissible in his eyes.[7] This is the first "concealment." But when he does still more wrong, then God becomes hidden from him to the point of the "concealment within the concealment." Then it is hard indeed to find Him. Yet through the Torah even such people can be stirred and brought to a knowledge of God. They can come to learn that there is hope for them also to return to the truth and draw near to God. For through the power of the true Tsadikim all men can draw close to God at whatever time, wherever they may be.   *(Ibid. 56)*

---

7.   Kiddushin 20a, 40a, Yoma 86b.

13.   There are places which are so low that they seem totally divorced from God. Yet it is precisely there that the most exalted life force is concealed: there are the "secrets of Torah." A person who has fallen far must know that in the very place where he finds himself he can achieve unique closeness to God because of the exalted life force which is concealed in that very place. When such a person returns to God, a very high revelation of Torah comes about: the "Secrets of Torah."   (*Ibid*.)

14.   There are times when a person feels the stirring to return to God. He wants to begin to serve God and to make the journey to the Tsadik who can guide him. At such a moment he has to face the full force of the evil inclination. It takes great strength and persistence to withstand this new evil inclination which seems to be born afresh at every turn. It can happen that someone has a great urge to make the journey to men of truth. He sets out with tremendous yearning. But as soon as he is on the way, his desire dampens. And at times, when he finally arrives and comes to the Tsadik himself, he seems to lose his desire altogether. All this comes about because as soon as he made up his mind to make the journey to the Tsadik he slaughtered the evil inclination he had had before. Now there is a new and far stronger evil inclination which is born afresh in him at every moment, "for the greater the man, the greater his evil inclination.[8]" It is a great thing to seek to draw closer to God. That is why it takes renewed

---

8.   Succah 52a.

efforts at every moment to fight this new evil inclination which keeps being born afresh with every passing moment.   (*Ibid.* 72)

15.   There are many different kinds of evil inclination. The common run of people have a very low sort of evil inclination. their desires are grossly materialistic. In fact, they are quite nonsensical. Anyone who has a clear head and can begin to form some slight conception of the true greatness of the Creator can see that such desires are mere foolishness and idiocy. For him even the trial of sexual lust is a kind of nonsense which takes very little strength to withstand. His own evil inclination is on a far higher plane because his own level is higher. He has begun to acquire an understanding of truth.   (*Ibid.*)

16.   Higher still is the level of those whose evil inclination is a "fine husk." Such an evil inclination is only sent to a truly worthy man. But this is still not the level of the evil inclination of the true Tsadikim. Theirs is really a holy angel.

17.   The very strength of desire which a person experiences to draw closer to God can in fact be a danger thrown up by the evil inclination. At times his "passion" burns far more fiercely than it should. This is the meaning of the warning which God gave to Moses before the Law was given. "But let not the priests and the people break through up unto the Lord, lest he should break forth upon them". (Ex. 19:24). You must pray that God's loving-kindness will protect you from this.

(*Ibid.*)

18.   There are times when we experience God's strict justice. For example, when we have some serious problem or grave

misfortune, God forbid. Then is the time to be more steadfast than ever in escaping the snares of the evil inclination. For then it comes against us with full force. This is because the principal root of the evil inclination is in the divine aspect of justice.[9]   *(Ibid.)*

19.   Depression is a terrible scourge. It feeds the evil inclination. You should always take care to work on yourself to bring joy into your soul. There are many good ways of doing this, as will be explained later. Joy is the foundation of spiritual strength. As we find written "For delight in God, that is your strength." (Neh. 8:10)   *(Ibid.)*

20.   The approach to God starts with rejection. When a man wants to draw closer to God, he usually experiences all manner of hardships, harsh experiences and fierce obstacles. He starts believing that he has been rejected. But, in fact everything is for his own good. The purpose is actually to bring him closer to God. It takes great strength and determination to stand up to this trial and not to let yourself get pushed away by the hardships and obstacles and the sense of rejection. You should not make the mistake of thinking that everything is out to thwart you. You should realize that everything that comes upon you is only for your good. It is to encourage you to draw upon all the resources of strength which are within you, so that you will be able to come ever closer to God. The entire purpose of this rejection is only to draw you closer. *(Ibid.)*

---

9.   True justice would be to discern what is right from wrong. This cannot take place if there is no evil inclination to give the person his choice of right or wrong. (See Lekutey Moharan I—72).

21. One of the secrets of spiritual strength is speech. However low you fall, you still have the faculty of speech. You should use it! Speak words of truth: words of Torah, words of prayer and the fear of Heaven. You should speak to God. Speak also to your friend, and especially to your teacher. The power of speech is such that at all times it enables you to remind youself of the closeness of God, and so to bring strength to yourself, even in the places which seem furthest from holiness.   (*Ibid.* 78)

Speech is the "Mother of children" (Ps. 113:9). A mother goes everywhere with her children. She can never forget them, even if they are in the filthiest of places. In the same way the power of speech goes everywhere with a person, even into the filthiest of places. There, too, one is able to utter words of holiness. The faculty of speech will never abandon a person or allow him to forget God. Understand this well if you truly desire to acquire your share in the world to come. (*Ibid.*)

22. Always be joyful and serve God with joy. Even if at times you fall, you can strengthen yourself with the radiance of the light which shone upon you at some previous time. The new courage which the memory gives you can help you in your present condition.   (*Ibid.* 222)

23. A person who has to spend his time among the gentiles, because of his business concerns, for example must be extremely careful to protect himself from being harmed by bad influences. Without noticing it he can easily become trapped in their nets. It takes great steadfastness to bear in mind at all times the sanctity of his heritage as one of the Children of Israel. He must pray earnestly to God to grant that he should

not learn from their actions or their way of life.(*Ibid*. 244)

24.   The seat of strength is in the heart. A person whose heart is firm has no need to be afraid of any thing or any person. Such a one can achieve awesome feats and win mighty battles merely through the firmness and steadfastness of his heart. He is never afraid and he does not run from the sight of a fierce battle. So it is in the service of God. Understand this well.   (*Ibid*. 249)

25.   If a person falls from his level, he should know that it is something sent to him by the hand of Heaven. The whole purpose of the rejection is that he should be drawn closer. The reason for the fall is to awaken this individual so that he steps up his efforts to draw closer to God. The proper thing to do is to begin afresh as if you were just starting to serve God. Start now as if you had never begun before at all. This is one of the greatest principles in serving God. Every day, literally, make a completely new start.   (*Ibid*. 261)

26.   When a person begins to examine himself and he realizes how far he is from the true good, and how full of sins he is, he can easily fall to the point where he is totally unable to pray.

It is everyone's duty to search and search until he finds within himself some point of goodness. How is it possible that in all his days he never once fulfilled at least one precept or performed one good deed? But no sooner does he start examining this good which he did, then he begins to realize that even this good was "full of sores, there is no soundness in it." (Is. 1:6). The good was blemished and bound up with false motives. Still, somewhere in this little bit of good there must exist at least some "good points." Now the search must begin again — until he finds another good deed. Once again he finds that the good is mixed up with plenty that is dubious. But he must continue the search until he finds more "good points."

This is the way for a person to find the goodness and merit in himself. He emerges from the scale of guilt and enters the scale of merit. Through this alone a person can return to God. He can revive himself and bring himself to find a joy in himself, whatever his condition. Then he can pray with strength. He can sing and give thanks to God. (*Ibid.* 282)

27. Every person must take the greatest care always to follow this path. It is a fundamental rule of life for someone who wishes to draw close to God and not to lose his portion in the World to Come completely, God forbid. The essence is to remove from yourself every hint of the bitter blackness of depression. The fundamental reason why people are far from God is because of depression. They lose their morale, they come to despise themselves because they see the blemishes within themselves and the great damage which they do. In secret each one knows the soreness of his own heart and his private pain. People lose hope and they come to the point of total despair. Their prayers have no meaning for them and they can no longer serve God even in the ways they used to be able to.

Think deeply about this. Many souls are sunk because of depression. Despair is the worst thing of all. Stay firm in this path of searching for the good points which are to be found at every moment and in every thing. This is the way you can always bring new life and strength to yourself. This way you can come to pray with yearning, with life, and with joy, at all times. You will be able to return to God in truth.   (*Ibid.*)

28.   No one should ever give up hope for himself, however far
he has fallen. Even if he is lying in the very pit of hell, he must
never despair of God's help. Even there he can draw close to
the Almighty. For the whole earth is filled with His glory. The
true Tsadik is only worthy of the name in virtue of his power
to restore to life even those who are fallen farthest and to raise
them up. He can give them new strength and courage. He can
rouse them and stir them up. He can reveal to them that
regardless of what may have happened, God is still with them,
near them, close at hand, and concerned in every way. For the
whole earth is filled with His glory. And this same Tsadik also
has the task of proving to those who are on the highest levels
they still know nothing of the true wisdom of the Almighty.
For: "What are all your searches, what are your
investigations?"[10]   (*Likutey Moharan* II:7)

29.   There are many ways you can fall. Indeed, at times there
are people who go into a truly appalling decline. They fall into
the most squalid situations — what our sages speak of as "the
filthy places."[11] Such people are racked with doubts and filled
with bizarre and loathsome thoughts. They are beset by
confusion, their very hearts palpitate. This is because of the
kelipot, the husks, which surround and contort the heart,
throwing it into turbulence. It may seem to such people that
they will never find God. But there *is* hope — if only they will

---

10.   Zohar I—1b.

11.   See Berachot 24b. The reference is to unclean places where it is
forbidden even to speak words of Torah. The analogy is to the lowest depths of
where a soul can fall, God forbid.

steel themselves to search for God and beg for His help. They must cry out: "Where is the place of His glory?" Indeed, the further you think you are from God, the more you must force yourself to hunt and search for Him: "Where is the place of His glory?" You must pine after His glory, you must howl for it, strain yourself to scream and beg: "Where is the place of His glory?" Through this alone you will come to ascend to the very greatest heights. You will be worthy of rising to the level of "Where?" — "Where is the place of His glory?" This is the level of the most exalted holiness.

It is the essence of the return to God that you should search at all times and beg: "Where is the place of His glory?" Then the fall itself is transformed into a great ascent. The whole purpose of the fall is revealed as being solely for the sake of the ascent, as all our sages have explained in our sacred writings. Search into this idea and understand it well; it is very deep.   (*Ibid.* 12)

30.   Obstinacy is one of the main requirements if you are to serve God. Understand this well. Every person who wishes to enter the service of God, even the most insignificant of men, will inevitably have to endure innumerable ups and downs. He will find himself thrown down and cast aside in every conceivable way. To endure all this takes endless fortitude. At times the only way to strengthen yourself is with sheer obstinacy. Nothing is more vital than this obstinacy. Remember this well, for you will certainly need it in your quest.   (*Ibid.* 48)

31.   Know that all these falls and descents, all the confusions and destructions, are an inevitable preliminary to entering the

gates of holiness. All the true Tsadikim and all the truly God-fearing have endured all this.

You may be so far from God that you imagine that your every movement is a blemish before God. In that case, you should know that when someone is so deeply sunk in the grossness of the world, every single gesture and movement which he makes to extricate himself little by little from his grossness, is more dear and precious in God's eyes than words can describe. Even the faintest motion such a person makes to draw himself out of the grossness causes swift running in the upper worlds over thousands upon thousands of miles.[12]

(*Ibid.*)

32.   Use every ploy you can think of to bring yourself to joy. Depression does tremendous damage. Make every effort to rid yourself of it completely. One way is to search within yourself until you find the "good points". Another thing: remember the words of the morning blessing: "You did not make me a heathen." But for many people, the best way to come to joy is through jokes and laughter.   (*Ibid.*)

33.   Know that man in this world has to pass along a very narrow bridge. The main thing is not to be afraid.   (*Ibid.*)

34.   Reflect on the utter exaltedness of the Holy One, blessed be He. You will see that even for the slightest inappropriate movement or impertinent thought on the part of a man, viewed against the light of God's glory, should cause that man to deserve a penalty, God forbid. But God is filled with love, and the whole creation is filled with His kindness. God desires

---

12.   See story page. 123.

the world greatly. "Be strong and of good courage and trust in God".(Ps. 31:25). For He will not abandon you. Everything which comes upon you is for your own good. Depend upon God's abundant love, for it is without end. "God is great: And His greatness is unsearchable." (Ps. 145:3)

In the end a way will be found to turn everything to good. All sins will be transformed into merits (Jer. 50:20, Is. 1:18). Only "be strong and of good courage."   (*Ibid*. 49)

35.   Having the evil inclination is actually something of great benefit to us. It is with this that we can truly serve God. When we are subjected to the fierce heat of the evil inclination, we have the capacity to steel ourselves to get the better of it. Then we can channel this passion into an act of genuine service. If a man lacked the evil inclination, all his service would amount to nothing. That is why God allows the evil inclination to do its work and to infect everyone to such a degree, none more so than the ones who genuinely yearn to draw close to God. It is true that the onslaught and sickness of the evil inclination can reduce people to terrible lows and bring them to much sin and wrongdoing. But in God's eyes, all this is good and fitting because of the preciousness of those stirrings and gestures which a person makes when he is beset by the full force and power of the evil inclination. Even so he stirs himself to escape from it. Through this simple gesture of determination, he accomplishes more than he would if he were to serve God for a thousand years without the evil inclination.

All the worlds were created only for the sake of man, and his entire value and importance lies precisely in his having the evil inclination. His task is to strengthen himself to fight it.

The more forcefully an evil inclination attacks someone, the more precious in God's eyes are his efforts to fight it. Then God Himself comes to his aid, for it is written (Ps. 37:33) "God will not abandon him to its hand" — to the grasping hand of the evil inclination.   (*Ibid.*)

36. Every moment of the day the evil inclination attempts to overpower us.[13] It fans the desires, even if we refuse to pay attention to it and look determinedly in the other direction. Still it comes back and bites us again, a third time, a fourth and more. We must stay firm and obstinate. We must be absolutely determined that under no circumstances will we turn our attention toward the evil inclination. In the end it will be lifted from us and it will totally disappear. The same is true of the irrelevant thoughts which persist in coming to confuse us when we are trying to pray. The same thought comes into mind over and over again. What we need is firmness. Pay no attention to the thought whatsoever.

37. At the very moment when a person is rising to a level of greater holiness — for example when he is drawing closer to a true Tsadik — it can happen that all of a sudden he experiences something which is the very opposite of pure. Don't lose heart because of this.[14] It is a sign that you are coming closer to holiness. It can be a great good.(*Ibid.* 117)

---

13. Kiddushin 30b.

14. One of the ten miracles that occured in the Holy Temple (Avot 5:5, Yoma 21a) was that the High-Priest never had nocturnal pollution on the Day of Atonement, so that he shall remain pure for the services he had to perform that day. Considering that he was held to a minimum of food and drink, and wasn't permitted even to sleep, (See Yoma 18a&b) what is the miracle? Rabbi

38.   Despair must be totally ruled out! When a person begins
to realize how far he is from God, even if he feels he is at the
farthest extreme from God, this should not be a reason for
despair. On the contrary, it should be his consolation: through
this he can revive himself. For now he is conscious of his
distance. He might have been so far away that he would not
even have been aware of the fact, but now he acknowledges it.
Far he may be, but his very awareness of this is dear in the eyes
of God. This in itself should give him strength and life.

39.   Everyone in the world derives his life from the Torah.
The simple and the sinners, even the gentile nations of the
world — for everyone the source of life lies in the Torah. You
may be someone who for a particular reason is completely
unable to study the Torah. It could be that you find yourself in
a situation which will not allow you to learn. You should still
know that your life source is in the Torah. Even when a person
is forced to neglect the Torah, even if he is not able to learn, he
should still strengthen himself as much as possible in the fear
of Heaven. It is through the great Tsadik that the world draws
life from the concealed Torah. At times such a Tsadik may
himself lead a perfectly simple life.   (*Ibid*. 78)

40.   Through the true Tsadik there is hope even for a person
who has fallen to the lowest pit of hell. Through the hand of

---

Nachman explained: "The High-Priest had to enter the Holy of Holies, a place
that even he was forbidden at any other time to enter, due to its holiness.
Therefore, many obstacles were placed before him from the "other side" to
deter him. Hence the greatness of the miracle." Said Rabbi Nachman:
"Should a person feel bad and angry that a miracle such as was wrought to the
High-Priest on *Yom Kippur* was not performed to him?"

the Tsadik every person in every situation is able to draw life from the holy. Despair is totally ruled out! Wherever you have fallen, strengthen yourself in whatever way you can. There is still hope that you can return to God. "From the belly of hell I cried out." (Jo. 2:3). Even the cry from the lowest pit of hell is never lost. Cry and cry but don't despair! You must cry and beg before God all the time until in the end God will look down upon you from the Heavens.   (*Ibid.*)

41.   Even in the lowest pit of hell we can become close to God.   (*Ibid.* 112)

42.   If you believe you can break something, have faith that you can repair it.

1.   At times a person can reach the very gates of holiness. But then he falls away. All the forces of "the Other Side" — the Evil One himself — array themselves against him with tremendous force and refuse to let him enter the gates. He feels crushed. He may give up completely. But this is the way of the Evil One and the forces of "the Other Side." A man gets close to the gates of holiness. He is on the verge of entering. They spy him and they hurl themselves against him with all their force. It takes tremendous strength to stand against them and hold your ground. If you slip or fall or feel confused, you should pay no attention. Be strong, fight back, and do what you can to serve God.

It may take days, it may take many years. In the end be assured that with the help of God you will enter the gates of sanctity. For God is filled with love; He longs for our service. Every twist and turn, even the faintest motion which a man makes to draw himself inch by inch from the grossness of the world toward the service of God — all are collected together. Every step, every gesture, every movement is gathered up and they are all bound together. They all come to help him at the very moment he needs it most in his time of trouble.

(*Likutey Moharan*, II : 48)

2.   Serve God with all your strength and rely completely on His infinite love. He will never abandon you regardless of what you may have done in the past. The past is nothing, what counts is the time from now on. Simply don't repeat what you did. When temptations come, remain detached and control yourself. This applies to actions and also to thoughts. The thoughts of men have as much power as their actions. What you think counts, even in the world which we inhabit — that is, the "World of Action."[1] That is why you need to control your thoughts as well as your actions. From now on you may have to endure all kinds of situations. Don't get put off; simply don't pay any attention. Try not to feel it at all! It is inevitable that all kinds of situations will be sent to you precisely to help you achieve perfect repentance. For this you have to be exposed to the very same situations that you were involved in before. Only this time you mustn't be swayed. You must control your inclinations and avoid any of the old thoughts and actions. This is the essence of perfect repentance.   (*Ibid.*)

---

1.   The *Kaballah* speaks of four transcendental worlds, *Atzilus* (Emanation), *Beriah* (Creation), *Yetzirah* (Formation), and *Asiyah* (Action or completion), alluded to in Isa. 43:7. See *Pardes Rimonim* 16; *Etz Chaim, Shaar K'lalos ABYA*.

3. You will rise and fall hundreds and thousands of times before you merit to serve God perfectly. The greatest Tsadikim have also endured all this. The most important thing is your determination. Let nothing in the world distract you. Never go slack. Only serve God, whatever happens. The main thing is never to despair. You should always make a fresh beginning as if you have never begun before in your life. Start serving God *now* as if this is the very first time. Even in the course of a single day, you may have to start all over again from the beginning any number of times.   (*Ibid.*)

4. A person sees that he has been praying and begging, entreating and supplicating that he should be worthy of drawing closer to the service of God. But still after all this time there is seemingly not the slightest responses. He begins to think that no-one is listening, as if he is deliberately being rejected from God's service, as if he is completely unwanted. He loses heart and be begins to look down on himself. He starts slackening his efforts to serve God.

This person should be ashamed of himself for questioning God's ways. He should remember God's attributes. Truly He is "gracious and full of loving-kindness" (Ex. 34:6). To be sure, it is his wish that this man, too, should draw close, that he should steel himself and start all over again.   (*Ibid.*)

5. The more strongly a man yearns to come close to the service of God, the more the Evil One throws himself against him in an effort to put him off. It is like when two men are fighting. One of them sees that the other is coming against him with extra strength. So he hurls himself against his foe with all his force in an effort to throw him down. As soon as

some good is stirring in a man, the Evil One knows instinctively and gears himself to strike against him. You have to be canny in this. Use every ploy in the battle against evil.   (The Wisdom of Rabbi Nachman)

6.   There are times when a person imagines that he will never merit the life of the world to come because he is so distant from God. Still, he should be strong and determined. He should long for God, pine for Him, and do everything he can to serve Him in joy. Show willingness in your service. Show that you will serve God every moment, every day of your life, even without the reward of the World to Come. Even if you are certain that you will still be condemned to Gehinnom, all the same, God forbid, you must still do your part. Busy yourself with serving God. Grab a good deed here, a prayer, or a snatch of Torah there. And God will do what is good in His eyes.

7.   Perhaps you have not reached the point of truly serving God. You can still "wait for God." As it is written (Ps. 31:25) "Be steadfast, strengthen your hearts, all those who wait for G-d." Let nothing in the world throw you, because there is no worse evil than despair. You should encourage your friends so that they too will let nothing bring them to despair. You can still give encouragement to your friends, even when you know in the secrecy of your own heart all the problems which are afflicting you. It is easier to encourage your friends than it is to strengthen yourself, for "One who is tied up cannot release himself."[2] You may know in yourself how far you are from the

---

2.   Berachot 5b, Nedarim 7b, Sanhedrin 95a.

service of G-d, but you can still give all kinds of support to your friends. You can revive them and restore their souls. And through this it may come about that you also will be worthy of returning to the service of G-d.   (*Ibid.*)

8.   In some cases people draw close to G-d's service for a time but then they fall away. Even so, that brief time of closeness is precious indeed in the eyes of G-d, despite what may happen later.   (*Ibid.*)

LEKUTEY HALACHOT

1.(3)   When a new illumination of Godliness is sent to a man,
or when he experiences a fresh awakening toward God, the evil
forces are resentful. Now is the time that he needs strength.
On no account should you fall or allow your resolve to be
weakened, even if the same thing happens ten thousand times
or more. Your strength lies in the Torah. When you study,
create new concepts of Torah. If this is something beyond your
capacity, you can still strengthen yourself by making a new
effort to study and follow the ways of the Torah. Do so with
simplicity and *purity.* Be sure never to leave the paths of
Torah. True, all the passion and yearning in your heart is to be
holy, disciplined and detached in the vanities of this world in
order to be worthy of the radiant light which is dawning in
you. And certainly it would be a great thing to achieve such a
level. But the evil inclination is resentful and wants to attack
you. Don't let yourself fall because of this. "Be not over-
righteous and do not commit great evil." (Eccles 7:16, 17) You
can come to great harm, God forbid, if you overstretch
yourself when you are trying to reach holiness, and as a result
you fail. The best thing is to follow the paths of Torah with
simplicity. Then you can go on your path securely. Let your
eyes be closed to this world. Nullify yourself before God. If
you are able to achieve this and you pay no attention to the
vanities of this world, well and good. If your can't, in any
event, do not allow yourself to be disheartened. Just try to be

honest and to follow the way of Torah with simplicity. The
Torah itself will break and destroy all the forces of "the Other
Side" which strive to attack us and thwart us. (Laws of washing
the Hands in the morning 4:16)

2.(4)   Whatever a man's place, that is the place where he
must entreat God. The place where he stands — "where he is
there" (Genesis 21:17) — this man must elevate this place and
connect it with the One who transcends place. This is God,
who is the "place of the world." Then this man can serve God
in truth. There is no *place* which can prevent him. Through sin
you can fall to the "place which is not good," to the lowest,
grossest, filthiest place. Even there, remember God. For He is
the "place of the world." In Him there is place for all.
Therefore there is no such thing as a fall. In all the places
where a man is driven he can still return to God. "And from
there you will seek the Lord your God." (Deut. 4:29) From
there! From the place where "He is there." (The Laws of
Tzitzis 3:9)

3.(5)   Man's activity is bounded by space and time. It is here
that the forces of "the Other Side" have their hold. But God
Himself, is beyond space and time, in a realm where there is only
good. Here the forces of "the Other Side" have no hold at all.
Here everything is sweetened. "If I ascend to the Heavens, there
You are. The days were formed but the One is not among them"
(Psalm 139:8, 16). It follows that there is no place or time to
which we can try to flee from God. Despair is totally ruled out.
The reason is that *all* places in the world are close to God.
Beyond all places, He gives life to them all. He sustains

all the places and all the levels in the entire creation. The same is true in the case of time, so in every place and in every time we can find God. Place and time are both included in Him. They are only emanations of God. And by returning to God we ourselves can transcend place and time!   (*Ibid.* 15)

4.(6)   Every moment of the day we are wracked by confusion, desires, corrupt and bizarre thoughts, and worse troubles. They trouble us in all ways, never more than when we are trying to pray. To withstand it all you must be slow to anger. This is really an aspect of faith. You must have perfect faith in God Almighty, in the true Tsadikim and in the righteous ones. Serve God with determination. And let nothing throw you or upset you or make you lose your temper. It is the Evil One who wants to weaken you and insinuate his way into your mind, to persuade you that there is no hope. Pay no attention. Steel yourself in your resolve. Despair is totally ruled out. You may have fallen countless times. Perhaps you gave up hope long ago. But you can still strengthen yourself *now* and begin completely afresh. Don't fall for the "old-age mentality" of the forces of the "Other Side." Every fall in the world comes from this "old-age mentality." A person thinks that he has already grown old in his sins. He feels they have become such a habit that they are second nature now and there is no way that he can escape from them. It isn't true. Every day, every hour, and every moment, man has the strength to renew and revive himself and to become a totally new creation. God makes new creations every day. *No one moment is like any other.* Strengthen yourself and make a completely new beginning. Even on the very same day, you may have to start again several

times. Whatever happened in the past, forget it completely.
Keep your thoughts directed to God. Begin anew as from *now*.
This is the meaning of being "slow to anger." You need to
have endless patience to endure all the confusions and the
obstacles, to let nothing distract you or make you lose your
temper. Whatever happens to you, with all your might make
God your strength. For God is filled with love at every
moment. The fountain of His kindness is never exhausted.

(Laws of Tefilin 5:6)

5.(9)   The whole purpose of a fall is often to prepare the way
for a spiritual climb. The intention is to give you a jolt in order
that you marshall all your strength and focus your entire
consciousness on serving God. For the essence of the service
of God is to find new life and new strength every moment of
the day.   (*Ibid.* 22)

6.(10)   Most people have a profoundly mistaken concept of
the very nature of their own existence. They do not understand
that the soul which they have been given is drawn from the
holiest source. They find it unthinkable that they themselves
might ever really return to God and lead a life that is truly
righteous and honest. You can hear this regularly as soon as
people start talking about a particular individual who is
noteworthy for his piety. For a moment there is a stirring in
their own hearts, and they too yearn to return to God. That is
the nature of the People of Israel: to be filled with yearning to
return and come closer to God. No sooner do these people feel
this stirring than they immediately stop short. "Well of course
I can hardly compare myself to such a person. He was born

that way. It is part of his make-up." As if to say that all the Tsadikim have achieved came only from the innate holiness of their souls inherited from earlier generations. The fact of the matter is that all the achievements of all the Tsadikim came about only through hard work and effort in God's service over a period of years and years. It was only through determination, steadfastness, prayers and entreaties that they were granted their spiritual heights.

Every single person can achieve the same. The choice is in your hands! You are free! "The crown of a good name is above the others."[1] It is because of the mistaken assumption which people have that their own lives are not rooted in holiness, that they do not trouble themselves to fight the way the Tsadikim fought. They are suffering from a mistaken identity which originates in the "Palace of Exchanges."[2] It was there that the baby prince was exchanged for the son of the slave in the Rebbe's tale of "The Prince and the Servant Boy who Changed Places." It was because the Prince assumed that he was merely a slave that he fell to the degraded level he did. He no longer knew whether he was a prince or the son of a slave. It is the same with every person who is far from God. This has never been more true than today. Our bitter exile has endured so long. Today the Evil One waxes stronger and stronger, to the point where innumerable people have fallen into total despair. They assume that they are totally unsuited to serve God. All this comes only from the artful insinuations of the

---

1. *Avot* 4:17
2. *Eitz Chayim*

evil inclination. The truth is that the soul of every Israelite is exalted and dear beyond measure. They are the "sons of kings" with the power to achieve the highest, most sacred level, no less than the greatest Tsadikim. For they too have endured strange thoughts and moments of weakness like these. But they were careful not to allow themselves to be pushed off course. They stayed firm; that is how they achieved what they did. Happy are they! And so we find it written: "And he lifted up his heart to the ways of God." (Chron. II 17:6). (Laws of the Morning Blessings 3:6; see also the "Thirteen Stories of Rebbe Nachman of Breslev." Jerusalem 1978).

7.(11)   One of our principal duties is to thank and bless God because He "chose us from among all the peoples and gave us his Torah". The mission of Israel and the gift of the Torah are a "unique treasure" (Exodus 19:5). These two things are fundamental principles of the Creation. They cannot be understood by human reason. The Guardian Angel of Egypt tried to complain: "Did not the Jews also worship idols ?"[3] But the bond of closeness between Israel and their Father in Heaven is a "unique treasure" to whch nothing in the world can compare. It is beyond the grasp of reason. The concept of this bond is connected with the "point"[4] which includes all the "points" to be found in each individual member of the

---

3.   Zohar II, 170b
4.   A literal translation of the word *nekuda*, this refers to the inner drive and spirit that the Jew is known to possess and what has carried him through the long years of exile.

Children of Israel. This comprehensive "point" is embodied in
Moses our teacher, peace be upon him. A part of him is hidden
in the soul of every Israelite. It is this creative "point" which
stands between the decree of "Destruction!" and Divine
"Favour". And it is this "point" alone which stands between
Israel and the nations. It is what enables them to ascend from
the evil of the seventy nations — from "Destruction!" — and
to enter the sanctity of Israel — "Favour." It can happen that
an Israelite may have fallen to a point of virtual devastation
spiritually. He can no longer distinguish between the holiness
of Israel and the uncleanness of the heathens. Yet he can still
find within himself this creative, holy "point." It is part of his
heritage as an Israelite. He may be unable to *feel* it within
himself. But it must be an article of faith that the mystery of
this "point" of Moses is concealed somewhere within him.
The more a person has fallen, the more he is in duty-bound to
praise and thank God for his portion, that he is from the seed
of Israel and "He did not make me a heathen." It is through
this sacred "point" within him that he will climb from
"Destruction!" to "Favour."

Do not succumb to despair and make the mistake of the
generation whch was condemned "because he said, 'Let us be
like the nations' " Our sages were referring to this mistake
when they said the destruction of the Temple and the exile
came about "because they did not first bless God for the
Torah."[5] The people of that age felt guilty because of their

---

5. *Nedarim* 81a

actions. How could they thank God for the Torah if they were not keeping it? So, they lost contact with the sacred "point" within them. They held themselves in contempt and fell into despair. But the more wrong a person has done, the more grateful he should be to God that he still possesses the inalienable heritage of the holy "point" which is concealed within him. He must seek out the "good points" which he still has. These can be found through drawing closer to the true Tsadikim. They are the Moses' who can stir us and bring out the radiance of the "holy point" within us. They sweeten all the harsh judgments and draw us from "Destruction!" to "Favour."[6]   (Laws of the Morning Blessing 5:7,8)

8.(12)   Shema Yisrael: "Hear O Israel, the Lord our God, the Lord is One." (Deut. 6:4). This is the declaration of our faith in God's Will. Everything is governed only through the Will of God Almighty. The essence of the precept to recite the Shema each day is that the Jew should fill himself anew with this holy faith every day. As our sages said, "Every day let these words

---

6. Destruction is   SHMaD   שמד — 344
    Moses is   MoSHeH   משה — 345
    Favour is   RaTZON   רצון — 346
    The numerical values are:
    Shmad — Shin ש=300, Mem מ=40, Dalet ד=4 = 344
    Mosheh — Mem מ=40 Shin ש=300, Heih ה=5 = 345
    Ratzon — Resh ר=200, Tzade צ=90, vav ו=6, nun ן=50 = 346
    Therefore Moses stands between destruction and favour to elevate all into favour before God.

be in your eyes as new."[7] We draw down upon ourselves this holy Will and bind to it our every thought, all the resources of our heart, our very being. At all times all our longing and yearning and desire should be only for the true, eternally enduring goal. The Jew strives every day to add afresh to the strength of this holy Will, regardless of what he may have to go through. He must never weaken his hold on this Will in any way. The essence of this concept it to believe that every day brings forth new creations; therefore, it is necessary only to wait with patience until the time the salvation itself will be revealed. Day after day God causes new salvation to blossom forth. Every day sees new holiness added from above. God has only one purpose in allowing the universe to endure — for "in his goodness he renews each day the work of creation". The purpose is to stir us, in order that we should renew each day our will and desire for God.

All this is connected with the Torah laws concerning cleanness and uncleanness. A person's purification was made dependent upon *time*. In some cases a person who was unclean had to wait only until sunset for the completion of his purification. For this person, salvation was linked with the coming of the new day immediately following his uncleanness. Others required seven days before they were purified. And when Israel came out of Egypt, they had to count seven weeks before they were ready to accept the Torah.

On each new day you must find added strength, for you

---

7. *Rashi* Deut. 26:16 *Tanchuma Yitro* 13, *Pesikta Zuta Ve'eschanan* 6

have not yet reached the perfection of purity, which only comes with accepting the Torah. And there are some, indeed, who do not reach the point of their perfection until after the sun has gone down completely: after they leave this world. "When the sun goes down, he is pure, and afterwards he may eat of the hallowed things" (Leviticus 22:7). These "hallowed things" are his share of the goods stored up in the world to come. He will win this good the moment his sun has gone down. He will have no need to return again to this world in a new incarnation and to endure all the torments of the people who fail to prepare themselves all the days of their lives — who fail to strengthen themselves in the holy Will day by day. For this person, when the last day comes, every snatch of goodness which he gathered while he was in this world, every gesture he showed of the will and desire for holiness — all will be gathered together to provide him with hope for his eternal good.   (*Ibid.* 5:41)

9.(14)   If you decide to take pity on youself and consider your eternal purpose, here is your entire remedy: Pay no attention at all to whatever you may be in your own eyes. Every day you are an entirely *new* creation. Man is created anew every day.

This is the reason we recite all of the blessings of thanksgiving every morning as laid down in the prayer book. The work which has to be done every day should seem completely new. Every Israelite has to fulfill numerous precepts day by day: *tzitzis*, *tfilin* and so on. In all this, concentrate on one idea. Today has never existed before, nor will it ever exist again. The task in hand is totally new. The duty rests upon *you:* this single person who is standing in *this* generation at *this* point in the whole of eternity. It has to be done by you. "Not an angel! Not a seraph!". Even the souls of the Tsadikim which repose in the upper Eden are unable to complete this task. "One like *me* will praise You today!" One like *me* on whatever level I may be — I am the one who has to praise you!

It is precisely the one who is most degraded and most low down who brings the greatest glory to God's name when he seeks to draw close. This is what our sages said about Jethro, who had experimented with every single idolatrous cult in the world. "When Jethro came and said: 'Now I know that the Lord is greater than all gods, then was His name glorified and magnified.' "[8] The essence of God's greatness is displayed when those who were far draw near to Him.

The one sure way to fulfill the Torah is to make a new start every time. This is possible even for people who think that they are not able to accomplish anything because of the tremedous force of the gross materialism which they feel trapped in. At least they can always *begin* to prepare themselves and start to get themselves ready to serve God. "I will be what I will be" (Exodus 3:14) — "I will fulfill what I am preparing to do."

You may have to make many beginnings even on a single day. Certainly, every week you will have to do so. But be

---

8. *Zohar* II 69a. See note 4 Pg. 14

assured that all the beginnings you make will be gathered
together. They'll all come to your aid when you really need it.
"There is not a good thought that is ever lost."[9] In the end you
will be able to complete the entire task and to find perfection.
Every day you must put out of your mind completely whatever
has happened until this very moment. Forget the repeated
beginnings you may have made in God's service as if they no
longer count for anything at all.

All the falls and the backsliding in the world come about
because people think that they tried once and it didn't work.
They lost heart, and they end up in total despair. Forget what
happened in the past. Even if you have tried hundreds upon
thousands of times... The essence is Now. Start now, afresh.
Prepare yourself to serve God with all the force which is in you
today. The task you have to fulfill now could be to cry to God
from the very depths of your heart. Or it could be to sit down
and open a book and learn. It could be to pray with fire. Or to
carry out one of the commandments of the Torah. Or to bring
yourself to joy because "He did not make me a heathen." The
same basic advice applies to all the various ways of serving
God. Start now — and in the end you will be able to fulfill the
entire Torah. You will achieve the most exalted heights. You
will be worthy of singing the song which is destined to be sung
at the end of time, the single — doubled — tripled —
quadrupled song which is woven from the four letters of the
holy name of God.[10]   (Reading of the Torah 6:17,30)

---

9. *Zohar* II 150b
10. *Tikuney Zohar* 21, *Lekutey Moharan* B Lesson 8

10.(18)   At times a person gets into a state of mind where he becomes suspicious of all the words of encouragement which the true Tsadikim and their followers have given: how "there is no reason in the world to despair, because however far one has fallen, God is still close by; He supports even those on the lowest level and longs for them to return to Him." People start thinking that none of this applies to their own particular problems, in spite of the fact that the Tsadikim explicitly assured them that it does. They start suspecting that the Tsadikim simply want to give them false assurances so that at least they will not slip any further. But they themselves have already been fully convinced by the Evil One that they have fallen so far that there is no hope left for them at all.

People who have joined the community of followers of the true Tsadikim live with a perfect faith in the guidance of the Tsadik. They are free of suspicion that his encouragement is groundless. The essence of the spiritual achievement of the Tsadik is to climb to the most exalted perception of the utter Love of the Almighty, blessed be He, a Love which is unfathomable and without end. The most cast-off of men is not cast off from the love of God. All the words of comfort of the true Tsadikim are not the inventions of their own hearts. They are the words of the living God, which He has made known through the agency of these Tsadikim and their followers who remained after their death. The message is the same: to know that God is still with us in every generation. That He will never abandon us, even when Jerusalem is rebuilt and established as the "praise of all the earth." (Is. 62:7) At the end of time we will merit seeing all this with our very eyes and "The glory of God will be revealed men. For the mouth of the Lord hath spoken." (Is. 40:5)   (Washing Hands before Eating 6:82)

11.(19)   All the obstacles and confusions which come upon a person who has started to return to God are derived from what we can term "the soiled garments." (Zechariah 3:4). One of the greatest frustrations comes when a person has already entered the path of self-purification. All of a sudden he falls, and all the old desires and impulses come upon him with an even greater force. All this comes about because of the "soiled garments," from which he is still not fully cleansed. It takes great efforts to succeed in stripping off these "soiled garments." Not everyone achieves this.

The reason for the return of all these desires and confusions can be understood when you consider the processes of sifting and purification which go into the making of bread, man's basic food. Before bread can be eaten, the grain has to undergo process after process. The land must be ploughed, the seed must be sown and harvested. The wheat has to be separated from the chaff. It must be ground, and the flour must be cleansed from the bran. All the waste that was attached to the grain is also an aspect of the "soiled garments," which have had a grip on man's food ever since the act of eating was blemished because of the eating from the tree of the knowledge of good and evil. All the processes of purification have the purpose of cleansing the grain from the hold of the "soiled garments." Even this is not the end of the selection process. The climax comes at the actual moment of eating.

The task now is to eat in sanctity and to bless God in truth and joy: because the pure goodness which is within the bread will sustain you in life, enabling you to give thanks and praise to God Almighty. Through this you will share in the Infinite Light of the Giver of all Life. Now, the waste that still clings to the food is turned literally into excrement. It would seem that all the processes of purification through which the grain passed up to this point are counted as nothing in comparison to this final cleansing at the moment of eating, the cleansing from the "soiled garments." So it is with all the desires and impulses and confusions which a man has to endure. He has already started the process of cleansing himself just like the grain which first had to be cleansed of the hay and the chaff. That in itself was no small task. But there still remains the task of separating the bran, and all the other processes which are required to make bread fit for human consumption. Even then, after all these processes are complete, there still remains the final cleansing at the moment of eating itself. When the individual reaches this moment, he still has not achieved a thorough cleansing. He finds that the obstacles and the barriers and confusions are greater than ever before. But now the "soiled garments" are finally being stripped from him. The final cleansing which comes at the time of the eating is at times the hardest of all. Then, the task is to select the true good and to discard the evil excrement, which are the *kelipot*, the husks and all the forces of the "Other Side." This applies to the cleansing of the individual himself. And it applies also to the cleansing of the Universe as a whole. This is the task of those who seek to serve God in the present era at the climax of this bitter exile, as we stand in the throes of the Messianic

Age. Now is the time of the final cleansing to prepare for the ultimate redemption. Accordingly, it is the time when the "soiled garments" grip with the greatest force. Now is the time for courage and steadfastness in following the guidance of the holy Tsadikim. The purification can come only through Torah, which, as our sages said is "like spreading streams" (Numbers 24:6). Just as streams draw a man up from pollution to purity, so do the words of Torah."[11] (Laws of Breaking Bread 5:5-7)

12.(20)   How many people stumble and fall just when they have nearly reached the very point of perfection? They have come as far as the gates of holiness by themselves. They could easily have entered already. But all of a sudden such a force of obstacles and confusion was let loose against them that they thought they would never be able to stand up to it. They were simply intimidated. The ony remedy for this is to be absorbed in Torah. A person should be very firm and never allow his study to become weak. Regardless of what one has to endure, he can always gain strength from the Torah. All the remedies and the purificaitons from the beginning of the world to the end of the world are contained in the sacred Torah. (*Ibid.* 28)

13.(21)   Brazenness is not always wrong. There is a brazenness on the "side of holiness." In fact the only way to be a true Jew and to serve God is by developing this brazenness

---

11. *Berachot* 16a

and stubbornness. Every single one of us has to endure endless ups and downs, reverses and backsliding. It takes stubbornness to stand in your place and never to relax in your service for a moment. Never is this more true than when you make the journey to the land of Israel, which is the source of all the holiness of the Jew. Here is the place to win the battles, but only through stubbornness will you succeed. The essence of the glory and joy which God has from Israel lies in the stubbornness of every single Israelite. He is thrown down time and again, but he stands his ground obstinately. Our sages asked "Why was the Torah given to Israel? Because they are brazen."[12] This is the foundation of all our service of God.

(Laws of Grace After Meals 4:12)

14.(24) The Tsadikim are the "chariot" of God. As every Jew returns to God and perfects himself, he too can join in the completion of the chariot. It is written: "And your people shall be all Tsadikim" (Isaiah 60:21). The main thing is that you should be strong in whatever confronts you. Before you can attain this level of inclusion in the chariot you must first encounter the "raging whirlwind," the "great cloud," and the "flaming fire." (Ezekiel 1:4). These are the *kelipot*, the "husks" — the forces of the "Other Side," which are the source of all the desires and obstacles, of all the abuse and contempt which a person must endure from his enemies. To withstand all this requires skill in the "running" and skill in the "returning"[13] so that you can achieve perfect repentance

---

12. *Beitzah* 25b
13. See Pg. 13

and be included in the community of the Tsadikim, the
"chariot" of God. The start of true repentance is when you
can hear yourself abused and still remain silent. This is what
humbles the blood of the left side of the heart.[14] To attain that
humility is the aim of the commandment of circumcision.
Now we can see why the Vision of the Chariot (Ezekiel 1)
began with the revelation of *HaSHMaL* (Ezekiet 1:4):

Abuse	is	Herpah
Silence	is	SHetikah
Circumcision	is	MiLah

Through the precept of circumcision you can achieve
perfect repentance. Through this you can attain the level of the
"chariot," and you will be worthy of being included in the Man
seated upon the throne.   (Blessings over Fruit 5:18)

15.(28)   When a person first starts to serve God, things
usually go reasonably well at the outset. He prays, he learns
Torah, he does what he can to serve God. If we compare the
stages of a person's life with the order of a single day, this
beginning stage is like the time of the morning service. Here
the underlying theme is God's loving kindness. Everything is
arranged in order: the passages dealing with the sacrifices and
the incense, the passages of praise and the psalms, the recital
of the *Shema*, the standing prayer, and so on. At this point

---

14. "A wise man's heart inclines him to the right, and the fool's heart
towards his left" (Eccle. 10:2). This is explained as the places of dwelling
of the two inclinations, the good on the right and the evil on the left.

everyone is able to serve God straightforwardly in accordance with the level he has reached. But after the end of the service, when the activities of the day begin, what usually happens is that most people fall from their level of devotion. God begins to test them and try them. And the Evil One rises up against them. All this is well known to anyone who has tried to enter the service of God. You need endless resources of strength to let nothing in the world throw you. And most of all you must fight against "constricted consciousness." This is the worst problem of all. The Evil One gets to work to persuade you that everything is hopeless, that you will never achieve true joy or sincerity in your prayer. The "afternoon," when we recite the Minchah prayer, is the time when the hold of "constricted consciousness" is strongest. The dominant theme of *Minchah*-time is the strict justice of God. This explains why the sages said: "A man should always be scrupulous about the Minchah prayer."[15] Now is the time that you must really fortify yourself. You should know that there is no end to God's greatness and loving kindness. He has the power to turn everything from evil to good. Through repentance, even your sins will be accounted as merits.[16]

What is true of the various stages of the day is also true of the whole life of a man. The days of a man's life are called "day." His leaving this world is called "night and "darkness." As it is written, "So long as the sun has not darkened." (Eccle.

---

15.   *Berachot* 6b
16.   *Yoma* 86b

12:2) When half of his days are over, he comes to the stage of "afternoon," the time for Minchah. That is when the Evil One comes against him forcefully.

"It is good for a man to take upon himself the yoke while he is young"[17] for "Youth is a wreath of roses." (*Lam.* 3:27). But even somebody who did start to serve God when he was young finds that he has reached the middle of his days and there is still much that he wants to achieve. The Evil One works with tremendous force to try to pull him from the path of life. All the more does it do so against someone who never started at all when he was young. Now he realizes that most of his days and years have passed. He wants to return to God. But the Evil One does his utmost to try to prevent him from leaving the lusts and desires in which he is ensnared. This is the cry of the Song of Songs: "Tell me, O Thou whom my soul lovest, where Thou feedest, where Thou makest Thy flock to rest at noon."(1:7)

When you are young, you should pray and entreat God that you never fall from His service. In the afternoon of a man's life, when evening begins to draw near, the danger is that he will fall into the "time of old age" (Psalm 71:9). He must take stock of himself and examine himself and his destiny. Now is the time to use all the strength at his command to sweeten the "strict judgments." These are the evil inclination and the hold of "constricted consciousness." He must bind himself to the true Tsadikim, the Moses' who can sweeten the "strict

---

17. *Shabbos* 152a

judgments" of Minchah-time at their source in the highest
world.   (*Afternoon Prayers* 5:5)

16.(30)   The sages said: "Nothing can stand before the power
of repentance.[18] It awaits a man until the day of his death." A
person may have sinned countless thousands of times. But
each time that he is stirred, even slightly, to return to God, not
a single impulse toward holiness is lost. In the words of the
holy Zohar: "There is not a good thought which is ever lost."[19]

The great power of repentance is that it can transform a
person's transgressions into merits.[20] What was damaged can
be restored. The reason for this is that the essence of the
transgression itself is to draw down the divine light into gross
and lowly places. The light then becomes enclosed and
concealed within thick vessels. But through repentance it is
possible to refine and purify these thick vessels so that they
will be capable of holding a new radiation of light. If the
transgression had never taken place, the vessels would never
have become thicker in preparation for their subsequent
refinement. In that case it would never have been possible for
the new radiation of light to reach these gross and lowly
places. Before repentance the new light still could not be
drawn down because the vessels were too thick to receive it.
But through repentance, the damage which was done by the
transgression was corrected, and the vessels were relined.

18.   *Devorim Rabbah* 2:15. See *Yerushalmi Peah* 1:1, *Zohar* II 106a, III 76a,
      122b
19.   *Zohar* II 150b
20.   *Yoma* 86b

without the transgression, there would have been no vessels to repair. Now that the transgression has taken place, repentance relines these vessels, and now the light can be radiated to places where it would never have been able to shine before. All this explains how the entire purpose of the descent is to enable the ascent to take place. Rejection from God is for the sake of being drawn closer.

But the restoration of the world which is brought about through all this can only be achieved through the power of the great Tsadikim. They are the ones who grasp the very heart of these mysteries. They know how to arouse people to return to God, and they are able to give them the encouragement they need. These Tsadikim can detect and work upon the "the good points" which are to be found in everyone. Through this they prepare unique vessels which make it possible for every individual to achieve his own ultimate fulfilment. Everyone should seek out such a Tsadik to work for his own redemption. Even the searching itself is a wonderful thing. In itself it can create enduring good, even for a person who has sinned a great deal. The greatness of the Tsadikim lies in the perfect manner in which they achieve the "arousal from below." Through this they fashion the most awesome vessels: through these vessels healing can come to the entire creation. Nevertheless, each individual still has to make his own arousal from below, for without this it is impossible for the necessary restoration to be made. A person must take the utmost care never to rebel or to speak words of abuse against the Tsadik who is working for his redemption.

The sages used remarkable language when they spoke about the greatness of repentance. "In the place where the penitents stand, even perfect Tsadikim cannot stand."[21] "Repentance reaches to the Throne of glory itself."[22] Through his sins, the penitent descended to the lowly places. But he braced himself to emerge, with the help of the Tsadikim. It was precisely because of the descent followed by the ascent that unique vessels were formed. These vessels could receive light of a kind which the vessels of those who have never sinned could not receive.

All this is possible only because of the strength of the great Tsadikim. They are the true penitents, the *Baalei Teshuvah* — masters of repentance. They never taste the taste of sin, but they still repent — from the levels they have already reached! And they intentionally lower themselves to the lowest places in order to elevate the souls which are there and to cause them to return to God. This is the meaning of the verse: "As for me, my hands are stained with blood... in order to cleanse."[23]

(Laws of Afternoon Prayer, 7:32,52)

17.(33)   All beginnings are hard! How is a person going to be stirred to return to God if there isn't a single spark of God's light inside him to wake him up? And how can God's light begin to dawn within him if he hasn't even started to return to

---

21. *Berachot* 34b, *Sanhedrin* 99a, *Zohar* I 39a
22. *Yoma* 86a
23. *Berachot* 4a

Him? For "no stranger shall eat of the holy thing." (Leviticus 22:10)

Where is the starting point? Even if God takes pity and radiates light into the depths of this person's darkness, he is already so broken and shattered by his sins that he cannot contain the light. For him any light at all is too strong. This is why it happens that at times a person may be stirred to return to God for awhile, but then he falls away. The same thing can happen several times in succession. The reason is that he still has not prepared the vessels that can contain the light stirring within him.

The same is true of the people of Israel as a whole. We have endured repeated exiles and redemptions. In the time of Joshua we entered the land of Israel and conquered it. But later on, we went into exile. Later still we returned for a time. Then came another exile. But all the time, "The right hand of God is held high" (Ps. 118:16) to eternity. Every time that Israel was able to return to the land, there were miraculous achievements in the work of reconstruction. Afterwards the Evil One returned and the Children of Israel relapsed and slid away. But the imprint of all that was accomplished remained — and it is still with us today. It is through the power of this residue that there is still life in us, even at the height of our present exile. Because of this we can still achieve flashes of spiritual vision.

So it is with someone who struggles in the service of God. He makes a start, then he falls away... he starts again and he falls again. He may even slip back completely, God forbid. Yet even the merest scraps of good which he succeeded in doing leave their imprint. These traces in themselves are something awesome. They too are essential for our present task, as we await the arrival of the Messiah. We are engaged in constructing a holy Building which will last to all eternity. The Building must include all the outcasts of Israel. They will all have to be gathered together and be united with a new holiness. Not a single outcast must remain outside. The purpose of this Building requires countless instruments and vessels. Every deed which any Jew accomplishes now, be it learning the Torah, a prayer, an act of charity or any of the other precepts — all are dear beyond words in the eyes of God. If someone has made an effort to serve God, then even if he later falls to appalling depths, not a single scrap of the work he had done before will be lost. Even a thought or the faintest stirring is never lost. As soon as they came into being the true Tsadikim snatched them and laid them in place ready to be included in this eternal Building. All these "scraps" bring great joy in the higher worlds. Every single one of them is crucial. Without it the Building could never be complete. It is the same as when nine men are waiting to pray. They may be the greatest Tsadikim. But being nine they are still short of the required quorum for prayer. They are forbidden to utter a single word of the communal prayers. All of a sudden some totally insignificant man comes in from the streets. Whoever he may be, he is joined to them. They are ten. Now they can recite the *kedushah*, the Sanctification. No sooner than they are finished, this same individual makes his escape and goes back to the streets. But the words of holiness which were uttered before can now never be erased. What joy they have

brought to the Holy One, blessed be He!   (Laws of the
Evening Prayer 4:34)

18.(36)   There are three husks which separate a person from
God. The first attacks him in the head. It enters him brain and
his mind with thoughts of money and the other desires. The
second gets him in the heart. It fans a burning sensual passion.
If there were only these two at work, he would still have the
hope that some good "point" would survive with him and help
him to master the passions of his heart and the thoughts in his
brain.

It is the third husk which is worst of all. It seeks to winnow
its way into a person's being, to demoralize him and throw
him into full-fledged retreat. "Why are you exhausting
yourself in the company of all these saints and pious figures?
Haven't you been with them long enough? It hasn't made the
slightest difference to your wicked thoughts and the lust in
your heart! It's no use! You'd be better off making money and
being like everybody else." This person has been working on
himself for ages, and he still sees no sign of progress. He may
even feel worse than before he started.

This husk is the worst because it wants him to go into
retreat. In fact, it is precious simply to spend time in the
company of honest, God-fearing people. He may feel worse
than he was before. But in his heart he knows the truth. It is
not being close to them which has caused all this torment. Had
he listened to their guidance and followed it, things would
have been good for him now and for ever. But the power of

freewill is great indeed. That is why he did what he did. Who knows what might have happened had he not been close to them at all? There is a sly one who waits in ambush all the days of your life.   (*Sabbath* 6:12)

19.(40)   The war against Amalek (Exodus 17:8-16) is the war against the evil inclination. It is a prolonged war. The way to humble Amalek is through strength. Regardless of what you go through, don't let anything at all throw you down. "And if I make my bed in hell, behold there You are." (Psalms 139:8). Even from there, when your strength is weak, you can still cry out to God. "From the belly of hell I cried out."(Jo. 2:3) This is the path back to God that we should follow during the Days of Awe, the ten days from the New Year to the Day of Atonement. The battle is against despair. So long as you refuse to succumb to despair, and you steel yourself to begin anew, you are called "victor of the war." The war is actually God's war. In the words of the Torah: "The Lord will have war against Amalek." (Exodus 17:16). God does the work. Man alone could never win were it not for the fact that God helps him. Man's task is only to strengthen himself all the time and to be sure never to retreat from the war. This is hinted at in the words of the holy Zohar:[24] "Who is the victor? The one that holds the weapons of the battle in his hand." So far, we cannot see clearly who is the victor in our long and bitter war, as the exile deepens for all of us. But so long as we grasp our weapons in our hands we are the victors. The weapon of the

---

24. *Zohar* I 221a

Jew is prayer. Cry out to God Almighty. This is our hope of victory.   (*Ibid.* 7:54)

20.(41)   The very devices which the Evil One uses to depress you can actually teach you how to have real faith. He insinuates his way into the soul with the thought that now that you've spoiled everything, there is no hope of repairing the damage and finding God. There actually are people who are fully aware of the damage they have done. Others have tried again and again to return to God, but each time they have fallen. The Evil One gets to work to persuade them there is no hope left.

But there is a way to make all these devices work for good. These thoughts spring from faith and from knowledge that there really is such a thing as sin. You *do* believe that sin causes damage in all the transcendent worlds. The concept of damage can only exist if there is also a concept of repair.[25]

The atheists and the philosophers of materialism try to deny the concept of sin. They say there is no such thing at all. They cannot accept that the prohibitions in the Torah are sins. That is why they are forced to produce all kinds of spurious reasoning to explain all the prohibitions away. They have to distort the plain meaning of the Torah.

Our faith as the holy nation is that there *is* such a thing as sin, which does indeed cause damage to all the worlds. It is this

25. *Lekutey Moharan* B, 112

very belief that we have caused damage that the Evil One tries to use to depress us. This is the first step in his campaign to drive us to total atheism. He wants to depress us to the point where we try to deny that what we did was a sin. "There is no judge, there is no justice."[26] "Today the Evil One tells you: 'Do such and such.' Tomorrow — 'Bow down to this idol.' "[27] All our backsliding comes from this demoralization which the Evil One puts in our minds. That is why we have to fortify ourselves with the faith that if there is a concept of damage there is certainly a concept of repair. The essence of all the precepts of the Torah is to bring us to faith and knowledge of "the One who spoke and the world came into being." If you have faith that you can repair the damage, it will be easy for you to return to God. You will give Him great pleasure through your work of repair in the very place where you find yourself now. All your sins will be transformed into merits. (Laws of the Sabbath Boundaries 5:26)

21.(45)   When things sink to the lowest point and the darkness is thickest, this is the moment of the "concealment within the concealment."[28] But this is actually the time of the greatest closeness to God. It is now that things begin to return to Him. For the darkness is God's own cloak as it were. "And I passed through the land of Egypt, *I* and not an angel, *I* and not

---

26. *Vayikrah Rabbah* 28.

27. *Niddah* 13b, *Shabbos* 105b

28. *Lekutey Moharan* A, 56. See Pg. 20

a seraph."[29] If a person were worthy of stripping off the cloak he could draw close to God Himself.

It takes wisdom to tell exactly when the ultimate pitch of concealment is reached. Without this wisdom the very thickness of the concealment can be overwhelming. The cause of the concealment is the great force of the powers of the "Other Side." Their strength comes from the "breaking of the vessels."[30] But this came about because of *too much* light. the pure Infinite Light was too powerful to be contained. It might appear that the hiding of the light is the worst thing in the world. God himself becomes hidden. But the concealment was necessary because of the very abundance of the light. It follows that the concealment itself must contain this awesome light. But only the very greatest sage is able to find it. The revelation of this light is the Exodus from Egypt.

It was in Egypt that the children of Israel descended to the lowest pitch of degradation. "Go down," (Genesis 42:2) said Jacob to his sons. The Hebrew word for "go down" is *redu*. The sum of the numerical value of the Hebrew letters is 210,[31] corresponding to the 210 years of the exile in Egypt. It was then that they fell to the lowest point. But Moses, our teacher, was worthy of attaining the wisdom that was needed in order

---

29. Passover Haggadah
30. *Eitz Chayim*
31. *Resh=200, Dalet=4, Vav=6 = 210. The 400 years of exile alluded to in Gen. 15:13 began with the birth of the Patriarch Isaac. See Rashi Gen. 15:13*

to strip away the cloak of concealment. He was able to transform the concealment into revelation. Through this, the Children of Israel were redeemed.

The sages of Israel have always been expert in the phases of the moon (of Exodus 12:2).[32] The sanctification of the New Moon at the beginning of each month is the revelation that is hidden within the depths of concealment. The moon corresponds to the *sephirah* of *malchus*[33] — the divine attribute of kingship. The waning of the moon is the concealment which comes about when the forces of the "Other Side" sap the strength of *Malchus*. This strength is derived from the light of the *sephirah* of *hokhma*, wisdom, which is drawn from the Source of all light. This is why the moon receives her light from the sun, which corresponds to *hokhma*.[34] It is precisely when the moon is closest to the sun and stands directly opposite it that she wanes to the point of total conealment. Then she gives no light to the world at all. When she reaches this point she immediately begins to wax again, and the new moon is born. It takes wisdom to determine the exact moment when the moon begins to wax.

The sanctification of the new moon was the first precept given to Israel (Exodus 12:2). It was given at the time of Exodus from Egypt, because the two things are one. On the

---

32.   *Shabbos* 75a. See also *Ketubot* 112a, *Lekutey Moharan* A #61

33.   See *Lekutey Moharan* A #1

34.   *Ibid.*

New Moon, the movement to return to God begins. It is then that the concealment is revealed for what it is. This is why the custom exists of holding a minor Day of Atonement of on the eve of the New Moon, in order to arouse ourselves to return to God. The moon is at the climax of its waning and concealment. This is precisely the time for closeness. (*New Moon* 3:3)

22.(49) How may "times" every Jew has to endure! Good times and bad times. These are the 28 "times" which are spoken of in the Book of Ecclesaistes.(3:1-7) Included are all the times and seasons and changes, the moods, circumstances, and situations which everyone of us experiences from the day of our birth to the day of our death. This was what King David was speaking about when he pleaded with God, "For in Your Hand are my times. Rescue me from the hand of my enemies, my pursuers." (Ps. 31:16)

It is the great Tsadik who teaches Torah and wisdom to Israel, who can give strength to each Israelite to stand firm through all the "times" and changes which he has to endure.

There is an answer for every time and for every situation. At one time, the answer may be to turn to Torah study, at another to say a prayer or to do a good deed. At one time it may be necessary to cry and beg and weep before God. At another time to be joyous and glad. There are times for speaking, other times for silence. There is also a time when what we need is to turn aside from our service. For at times,

"To neglect Torah is to keep it."[35] There are times when a person has to eat or sleep in order to preserve his body. At other times he has to converse with other people, in order to sharpen his wits, and so on.

Everyone must endure innumerable different "times." This is mentioned in connection with the death of King David: "...with all his reign and his might and the *times* that passed over him and over Israel and over all the kingdoms of the countries" (1 Chronicles 29:30).   (*Passover* 9:5)

23.(51)   One of the reasons why people give up hope is that they look at their own contemporaries and imagine them to be far worthier than they themselves are. It is true that it is an admirable quality to be humble-spirited before all men and to look upon everyone as if he is better than you. But if this makes you give up hope, you can be certain that you have not achieved true humility. On the contrary, there is a great presumptuousness in saying that you are not the right one to perform a certain act of service for God, because of your great distance from Him, in comparison with your friends. You must never make these kinds of excuses before God. Man is not his own judge. Who really knows what his true position is before God, or where his actions might take him? Every person is an individual in his own right. No-one can be compared to anyone else.

As our sages said, in connection with the counting of the

---

35   *Menachot* 99a, b

Omer, "And you shall count unto you" (Leviticus 23:13) —
and you shall count *for yourselves*.[36] The counting of the Omer
is the preparation for receiving the Torah. Each individual who
comes to cleanse himself has to do the counting for himself.

This is also the implication of the statement "Abraham
was one man."(Ezer 33:24) In other words, he always looked
upon himself as if he were the only one in the world. He paid
no attention at all to any obstacles or distractions. The
barriers in the world do not only come from the wicked, who
try to thwart us with temptations, mockery and opposition.
Obstacles and demoralization can come even from one's
closest friends and from people who are genuinely honest. It is
not possible to explain this fully in writing, but a sensible
person will be able to work it out for himself.

To fight against these barriers you must follow the path of
Abraham who "was alone in the world." Pay no attention to
what your friends are doing. "And you shall count unto you"
— count for yourself.

Always be joyful — even if you are poor and under
pressure, even when your service of God and your prayers feel
ragged. Always be content with your portion. Pay no attention
at all to the rest of the world. It may seem to you that other
people have an easy living and that their service of God, their
learning, and their prayers are a thousand levels higher than
your own, even though you never see them putting in the same

_____

36   *Ibid.* 65b

effort and toil that you have to achieve your own low level. Pay no attention to thoughts like this. Be content with your portion and with every good "point" that is in you. Give thanks to God that he made you worthy of this. What do you care that your friend is greater and better than you? God is good to all. This was the mentality of the simple one in the story of the "Simple One, Clever One." People would ask him why his business rivals got a higher price than he did, "What do I care?" he would answer. "What they do is their affair, what I do is my affair!" He took great joy in his own craft, even though his products were not perfect. He was overjoyed at the little profit which he made through the work of his hands. He paid no attention to anybody else. (*Ibid.* 9:11; the 13 Stories of Rabbi Nachman of Breslev, the Clever One and the Simpleton).

24.(52)   In the hour of a man's fall, a shield of the highest sanctity surrounds and protects him. "The mother hides her children."[37] This is the idea of the Tabernacle of Peace, the clouds of glory which surrounded Israel in their journey through the wilderness, with all its snakes, serpents and scorpions.

25.(55)   The essential truth of the whole universe is ultimately simple. All things were brought into being out of nothingness by the hand of the one Creator. To Him they are destined to return in the end, at the time when the universe will be renewed. When a person fills his whole being with this

---

37. *Tikuney Zohar* — foreward

truth at all times, falsehood can never have a hold on him.
Regardless of the uncleanness, evil, or falsehood he
encounters, he can always return to the sanctity of God. God
is to be found everywhere, at all times. "If I ascend to the
Heavens, there You are; and if I make hell my bed, behold,
there You are. For the darkness is not hidden from You"
(Psalms 139:8-12). When he keeps to this faith at all times,
there is no darkness, falsehood, evil or uncleanness in all the
world that can divorce him from God, His Torah and His true
Tsadikim. They are the essence of truth. The more insistently
the Evil One comes against him with falsehood and
deceptions, the more he can draw close to the truth. The
descent becomes the instrument of ascent. All falsehoods
themselves arise from the idea that all things have their
beginning and end in God. Everything is a unity: silver and
gold, tin and lead. Lead in Hebrew is *opheret*. That is the same
as dust, the Hebrew for which is *aphar*.[38] As it is written:
"Everything came from the dust." This is why it is possible to
falsify and say "This is that." Falsehood can substitute one
thing for another and "say of silver that it is gold." Falsehood
is cast down when each Jew finds in everything its source and
its destiny: God. God is the beginning and end of all things. He
is the essence of truth. This is how falsehood disappears from
the world.   (Marks of Clean and Unclean Beasts 4:25)

26.(56)   We are taught that man has free will. But at the
same time, God is the ruler of the universe. This seems to be a
paradox. In order to understand it, you must realize that there

---

38. עפרת — Lead   עפר — dust

are two levels of free will in the world. On one level is man's own free will. When men choose to carry out the divine commandments and to perform good deeds, they participate in the task of cleansing the creation by choosing good and rejecting evil. Man's actions thus have a profound effect in bringing the Creation closer to its perfection. These individual acts of free will on the part of man constitute the "arousal from below."

The second level of free will is that which is in the hands of God. At every moment God himself acts to draw the Creation toward perfection. This constitutes the "arousal from above" through which God Himself cleanses the creation, sifting the good from the evil. Yet ultimately these two levels of free will are not separate. They are both aspects of the same thing. The "arousal from below" sets in motion processes in the worlds above. Conversely, the power to cause the "arousal from below" to come about is only in the hands of God Himself. However it is part of our condition in our present life that we are unable to grasp or understand the way in which these two levels of free will are really one. And it is our very inability to understand it that is actually the source of our own free will.

If you live your life with simplicity, you will never be troubled by this paradox. "He who goeth in purity, will go in trust."(Pr. 10:9) Through simplicity and faith, it is possible for a person to observe the entire law of the Torah in all its details. He works on the assumption that the healing of the entire creation is dependent on himself alone — that is, upon the "arousal from below" which he stirs through his

observance of the laws of the Torah in all their details. And
even if he stumbles into sin or wrongdoing, he still does not
become discouraged. He has the strength to return to God
because he knows that there is an altogether higher level of
freedom, namely the "arousal from above." The regions above
can never be touched by any blemish. "If you sin, what do you
do to Him."? In the higher worlds everything finds healing; all
transgressions are transformed into merits through the return
to God. The thoughts of God are "very deep" (Psalms 92:5).
Even from acts of destruction God has to power to create true
healing. A person who knows this in his heart will remain firm
in his service of God, regardless of what happens.

If people are distant from God and fall into wrongdoing, it
is only because they do not understand about these two levels
of choice. There are the people who have not begun to serve
God, or who on the contrary, do the opposite. This is because
the evil inclination makes them believe that the influence of
circumstances is more powerful than that of free will. He
persuades these people that man has no free will at all.
Everything is dependent only upon the decision of God. Now
that God has rejected this individual, the argument runs, there
is no hope for him to change and return to God. This
conception of man as the victim of his circumstances is totally
false. It is designed to provide a justification for atheism and
wrongdoing, so that people will throw off the yoke. There are
many people who would never dream of seeking this kind of
philosophical justification for their way of life. They are
simply trapped in their own physical desires and sins. But at
root they too are under the influence of this line of reasoning

fabricated by the evil inclination. At the heart of the evil inclination lies atheism.

On the other side, there are the people who have already started serving God to some extent. If they subsequently experience a fall, they become extremely demoralized. Some give up trying to serve God completely because they see that they have made repeated efforts but none of them has been successful. This is frequently found among young people. Here, too, the evil inclination is fueled by a confusion about the two different levels of free choice. Only, in this case, it argues that it is *man's* free will that is paramount, as if *everything* is in the hands of man and there is no help from God at all. And now that the person in question has stumbled and spoiled things, the argument goes, he has shown that he does not have it within him to improve.

In order to live simply, we must have faith that everything is in our own hands, *and* that at the same time everything is sent to us only from God. It may be impossible to understand this. But though *living* this paradox in practice, you will never be far from God, nor will you ever fall. Certaintly we must serve God with all our strength, as if everything depends only on us. For "He has given the earth to the children of men" (Psalms 115:16). On the other hand there is no such thing as a real fall, nor is there ever any reason to give up — because God is the final source of all things. He arranges all things according to His will "You, Lord, are most high for evermore" (Psalms 92:8). "The council of the Lord stands for ever" (Psalms 33:11). None of the good that a person does is ever lost,[39] even if he himself thinks it must have been worthless, because subsequently he had so many problems.

The connection between these two levels of free will is incomprehensible. It is the same paradox that our sages discussed in the case of a small boy who was killed when he went to obey an order from his father. We are commanded to honour our father and mother "that your days may be long upon the land which the Lord our God giveth you" (Exodus 20:12). This boy's father told him to climb up a tree in order to fetch a bird's nest. He told him to be sure to send away the mother bird in fulfillment of the law of the Torah (Deuteronomy 22:7). We are told to fulfill this precept, in order "that it may be well with you and that you may prolong your days." The boy fell to his death. Where, the sages asked, was the length of days which the Torah promised? "In the eternal world which is altogether long."[40]

In the same way, there are many commandments where the Torah explicitly mentions a special influence in keeping us from sin and bringing us closer to God, for example, the laws of *tzitzis* and *tefilin*. Yet there are cases of people who dutifully wear *tzitzis* and *tefilin* and still find themselves overpowered by their desires. In the end they throw off the yoke and stop carrying out these precepts.

---

39. *Zohar* II 1506

40. *Chullin* 142a

We have to have faith that all the words of the sacred Torah and of our sages are "true, firm and enduring" (From the Morning Prayer). But there are many matters which it is impossible for us to understand perfectly. There is no doubt that the power of the commandment of *tzitzis* is strong beyond measure. The wearing of *tzitzis* can draw men away from the evil inclination and all their physical desires. As proof of this, the Gemara brings the story of the man whose *tzitzis* were spread over his face.[41] Nevertheless, not all men are equal. There are cases where people have fallen so completely under the influence of their evil inclination that even if they do wear *tzitzis* it is still hard for them to stand up against it. It is precisely people like this who should take the greatest care to wear *tzitzis* and indeed to observe all the commandments. At least they will be left with the merit of having fulfilled the precept of *tzitzis* and they will not lose everything. Most likely the merit of *tzitzis* will in the end join forces with the other good points which exist within them, and they will be worthy of conquering their evil inclination completely, because no good is ever lost.

In the relationship between the two levels of free will there are numerous details the significance of which is hidden from us. The purpose of their being concealed is to give men true freedom of will. We have to do our part regardless, to try to serve God every day of our life. If in spite of this we never become worthy of holiness and purity, still, not a single good intention is ever lost.

---

41. *Menachot* 44a

You may have seen in a particular book that fulfilling a particular commandment or following a certain practice has a special influence in a certain direction. Perhaps you find that even though you have carried it out, you have still not achieved what you hope for. On no account should you become demoralized. Who knows the ways of God? It could be that He needed you to fulfill this commandment or to do the good deed for an altogether higher purpose. For God's thoughts "are very deep." You should never question the ways of God or the words of the Torah and the words of our sages. (*Ibid.* 38, 41, 42, 48, 49).

27.(57) The lowest levels of the entire creation are what our sages called the "filthy places."[42] They are not able to receive their vitality directly from the revelation of God's glory. The whole creation was brought about only for the sake of this glory through the ten fiats of creation. But of the "filthy places" it is written: "And My glory I will not give to another."(Is. 42:8) The life force which keeps them in existence comes from a source which is concealed: the unspoken fiat of "*bereishis*" — "In the beginning." (Genesis 1:1). This source is the "Where"? — "Where is the place of His glory?"

A person who has fallen to these depths may in the end want to do something for himself when he realizes how far he is from the glory of God and sees that his place does not deserve the name "place" at all. A *place* is only worthy of the name when holiness dwells there, revealing the glory of God.

---

42. See Pg. 27 note # 11

God is called the "place" of the world. The "filthy places" are not places at all. "For all their tables are filled with vomit and excrement *without place*.(Is. 28:8)" And it is written: "And there is no *place*.(Is. 5:8)"

Someone who has fallen to such depths has no place at all. He is "A fugitive and a wanderer in the earth" (Genesis 4:12). When a man sins and distances himself from God, it is as if he made the world relapse to its primal confusion — "unformed and void" (Gen. 1:2). Having destroyed the world, there can be no place for him in the world. But in the end he can come to know the truth and to see the damage he has done. He realizes he has left himself no place in the world. He can take pity on himself and beg and entreat, "Where is the place of His glory?" Even places like these must really derive their vitality from God, but it comes to them in a heavily concealed way: "Where is the place of His glory?" By begging and searching for the glory of God it is possible to rise to the greatest level of all: the unspoken fiat of the creation. This is the level of "Where?" which is *beyond place*. The fall took him down to the regions *beneath* place, "unformed and void." Through his search and entreaty he rises *above* place. All his sins are forgiven. For it is from the level of "Where?", transcendent in holiness, that all forgiveness comes. "With Thee there is forgiveness" (Psalms 130). "*With thee*" is the level of "Where?" This is the place of the "Crown, the Thirteen Perfections of the Image" which are the roots of the thirteen attributes of mercy. It is through them that all forgiveness comes into the world.

---

43. *Zohar* III 130b

"If your sins were red like crimson they shall be as wool"
(Is. 1:18). The crimson here is a dye which was formed from
the blood of a worm. The "filthy places" are the "skin of the
worm." This is the strong hard husk which rises up continually
with the aim of consuming the world completely. This husk is
the source of all unclean creatures — worms, reptiles and the
like. For the Jew to eat these is strictly forbidden, because they
are totally cut off from the glory of God. "And My glory I will
not give to another."(Is. 42:8) Yet the person who is trapped in
the "filthy places" can still beg and search for God's glory and
receive forgiveness through the "thirteen perfections of the
image." Our sages said that these are alluded to in the concept
of wool. Although the sins were "red like crimson, they shall
be as *wool*."

All this helps to explain what our sages said regarding the
worms which grow in fruit when it has been picked.[44] They are
only like food when they have moved from their original place.
When a person falls to the "filthy places" and sees that there
is no place for him in the sphere of holiness, the vital thing is
that he should not move from his place or fall into despair.
There are innumerable cases of people who having fallen, give
up completely and move altogether from the sphere of
holiness. Having gone beyond the limits, they have tried to
make their own place divorced from all holiness. Once they see
that they are cut off from a share in the World to Come, they
swarm over the ground and wallow in *this* world. These people
are certainly unclean and completely "forbidden." They are the

---

44. *Chullin* 67b, *Yoreh Dayah* 84:4

abominable things which creep over the earth in the regions of uncleanness where the serpent has dominion. But it is possible for this "worm" — the person who has fallen to the "filthy places" — to stay in his place without moving. He should at least stay within the bounds of holiness.

There is no place anywhere that a person can flee and hide himself from God. "Whither shall I flee from Thy presence?" (Ps. 139:7) What can he achieve by going any further in pursuit of the desires of his heart? Things can only end bitterly, and he will still have to give an account, like one who "found great gain," drawing himself little by little from the forces of the "Other Side". It is better to stop now and to realize how far one is from God's glory. Then he can beg and search for God: "Where is the place of His glory?" The Torah tells us that at the end of the exile, you shall seek *from there* for the Lord your God" (Deut. 4:29) From there! Because the right thing to do is not to "move" and go beyond the bounds, rather to insist on not abandoning your "place." As King Solomon said, "If a commanding spirit rises up against you, never abandon your place."(Eccle. 10:4) In his search for God, you can transform your fall into a lofty ascent to a level which is entirely beyond place. The worm, *tolah* becomes an *olah*, an offering — the perpetual offering which atones for the sins of the day and the night[45] and humbles and crushes the husks of the worm.[45a] (A Law Concerning the Prohibition against Eating Worms 3)

---

45. *Bamidbar Rabbah* 21:19
45/a. *Sha'ar Hacavanot, Drush Tefilat Shacharit* 3, *Lekutey Moharan* A 28.

28.(63) "A woman of worth who can find? For her price is far above rubies... She is not afraid of the snow for her household, for all her household is clothed with scarlet" (Proverbs 31:10,21). The Hebrew word for "scarlet" is *shonim*. Our sages said, "Don't pronounce the word as *shonim*; pronounce it *shnayim*, which means "twice over."[46] Give and then give again! Open and then open again! Be strong and then be strong again."

Keeping the Torah takes obstinacy. If you do something good, repeat it. If you learn something, go over it again. Whatever you start, do it again to get used to it. Whatever you do that is holy, do it again and again, repeat it even a thousand times. Repeat it even from sheer obstinacy. Pay no attention whatever to the subtle persuasion and insistent demoralization of the Evil One and your other opponents.

If you strengthen yourself in this way you have no need to fear the hell of snow. There are two hells, one of fire and one of snow. The hell of fire is for people who burn with the passion for lust and transgression. But the hell of snow is the penalty for demoralization. People are filled with regrets. Demoralization is the greatest obstacle to returning to God. People think that they have sinned so much that repentance won't help them. They give up all hope of drawing close to God. The hell of these people is cold and bitter: the hell of snow. Don't become cold in your pursuit of the Torah and of God is commandments. "She is not afraid of the snow for her household, for all her household are clothed with scarlet." (Meat and Milk 5:27, 29)

---

46. *Erchin* 10b, Yalkut Mishlei 31.

29.(68)   The greatness of God's love and tender mercy is inconceivable, and totally without limit. Even at the moment when He is at the peak of His anger, He still longs for us to turn to Him and pray. He yearns to send us His redemption, which is the only true salvation. That is why we must force ourselves to pray and entreat before him even when we feel the harshness of His anger. We must still trust in His abundant love and tender mercies. We will never be able to understand their true greatness. Even Moses forced himself to pray in this way. When Israel had sinned with the golden calf, God said that He would destroy them. Moses realized that he should pay no attention to the literal meaning of God's words. He spoke in that way in order to stir Moses to even greater heights in his prayer that God should sweeten the decree and silence the accusers of Israel. Moses prayed and pleaded fervently until he found favour with God. "And the Lord relented of the evil which he thought to do unto His people" (Ex. 32:14). It was then that God taught Moses the prayer of intercession and He revealed to him the thirteen attributes of loving-kindness. (Ex. 34:5-8). The essence of the revelation was that God's love and tender mercy are eternal and they will never cease. This is the meaning of the words which God spoke: "Merciful and gracious, long suffering and abundant in goodness and truth" (Ex. 34:6). God will always listen to our prayers, our entreaties and cries. Even if we make God angry because of what we do, His anger always comes to an end, while His love endures and remains for ever.

"The Lord is close to all who call upon Him, to all who call on Him *in truth*" (Ps. 145:18). "But as for me, let my prayer be to You Lord at an acceptable time. O God in the abundance of Your mercy, hear me in the *truth* of Your salvation" (Ps. 69:13). The "truth" which King David speaks of here is this: "Even now, after doing what I have done and going through what I have been through, I still believe with perfect faith that it remains your desire to save me. Therefore I will be firm, and pray. Answer me in the truth of your salvation." Make sure you understand this well. Ponder the meaning of this guidance and follow it. At all times be strong in your prayer, regardless of who you are.   (Laws of Interest 5:33)

30.(69) All the wars in the world are really the one war against the evil inclination. Even the battles which a person has to fight with his various opponents and enemies in the material world are in essence the war against the evil inclination. Our sages said, "Corresponding to a person's enemies in the lower world are enemies in the worlds above."[47] The war that has to be fought is the war against the evil inclination.

Before the Children of Israel went into battle to fight the wars of God, the priest would address them to give them encouragement. The fight of the Children of Israel was against the forces of the "Other Side," which are like a shell surrounding anything holy. Thus it was that the land of Israel was surrounded by heathen nations, and so it is that there are all kinds of barriers and obstacles in the way of anything holy.

---

47. *Sanhedrin* 44b, (103b)

As soon as a man wishes to fight these barriers, powerful accusers rise up against him and seek to throw him down completely in order to prevent him serving God. This is the time that he must stand on his feet and fight them with all his strength. So long as he doesn't relax his efforts to serve God, he will win the battle and break down all the barriers.

The source of his strength in this battle lies in faith. With faith, there is no need to fear any battle or test in the world. This is what the priest said when he spoke to the armies of Israel. "Hear O Israel, you draw nigh this day unto battle against your enemies. Let not your heart faint; fear not, nor be alarmed. Neither be ye affrighted at them" (Deut. 20:3). Our sages commented that when he said "Hear O Israel — *Shema Yisrael* — to the assembled army, what he meant was: "Even if you have no merit other than your saying twice every day, 'Hear O Israel, the Lord our God, the Lord is one,' even so, you would still be worthy of victory against your enemies."[48]

The foundation of our entire faith lies in the affirmation of God's unity which we make when we recite the *Shema*. Through this faith alone, you can win every battle, material or spiritual. If you are firm in your faith in God, there is no battle that can make you afraid.

"Let not your heart faint; fear not nor be alarmed. Neither be ye affrighted at them". On these words our sages

---

48. *Soteh* 42a

commented: "You should not be afraid of the galloping of the horses, the thud of the boots of the soldiers, or the noise of their trumpets. These are all tactics which the enemy uses to try to strike fear into the heart."[49] The same tactics are used in the war with the evil inclination. Everyone knows that as soon as he wants to serve God and fight his evil inclination, immediately the Evil One works to frighten him. He makes the service of God seem excessively difficult and burdensome. Plenty of people get put off by this — the galloping of horses and the stamp of hobnailed boots. To serve God you must have no fear at all.

In this world man has to pass over a very narrow bridge.[50] To get across it, you have to be without fear. Your strength comes from your faith "Hear O Israel, you draw nigh this day into battle against your enemies." But through the merit of *Shema* nothing will make you afraid. "The Lord is with me. I will not fear."(Ps. 118:6) You can have perfect faith in God, because the whole earth is filled with His glory. He is with you always. "I will have no fear. For what can a man do to me?". Through faith you can win every battle. In the end you will be worthy of returning to God in truth. "This is the answer I will give to my heart. Therefore I will hope." (Lam. 3:21) (Laws of Shaving 3:9)

31.(72) In this world people can never have a true understanding of their position or what they are faced with.

---

49. *Ibid.*

50. *Lekutey Moharan* B #48

This ignorance is actually the source of free will. It *is* the trial. If you want to succeed, you need faith. *You must also have faith in yourself.* You must realize that not a single movement you make in the direction of good is ever lost.

32.(73)   Consider the idea of time. Everyone knows how time gets wasted. Time moves on and flies away, and there is never a moment's rest. But you should look at all this through the eye of truth.

In reality there is no such thing as time. Time is only an illusion which comes about through the constriction of our consciousness. You can see this in the case of a person who is asleep. In the space of a quarter of an hour he has a dream. In the dream it seems as if seventy years have passed. This is only because of his constricted consciousness while he was asleep. As soon as he wakes up he sees with his own eyes that no more than a quarter of an hour has passed.

The same is true of our whole life. Our notions of time are pure illusion. Someone who thinks about this carefully will certainly put all his strength into abandoning the vanities of this time-bound existence and putting all his hope in that which is beyond time.

You should have faith in the One who is beyond time. Then nothing in the world can throw you down. Wherever you are you will always be able to remind yourself "This day have I given birth to you" (Ps. 2:7). These words refer to *Mashiach* who is in a realm beyond time. There everything finds healing.

Time past is annulled completely. The great Tsadikim, who are filled with the spirit of the *Mashiach*, are able to achieve this level beyond time. There is only today. Today you were born. Literally!

All that is wrong with the world is part of the "Evil work that is done beneath the sun" in the time-bound world. A person may want to cleanse himself from his corruption and return to God in truth. But what remedy is there for all the days and years, all the *time* that he wasted in wrongdoing? His only hope is in the realm beyond time. From there comes all healing. It will be as if he were born again today. So long as you have faith — in God, in the World to Come, and in the Messiah who is *beyond* time — you have eternal hope.

Our sages said of the proselyte who comes to convert: "He is like a new baby that has just been born."[51] He may have been brought up surrounded by heathen corruption. Even so — "I have *this day* given birth to you." Because now he has come to enter the Holy People. How much more does this apply to the *baal teshuvah* — the "master of repentance.'" He was actually born into the Holy People regardless of what may have happened afterwards. When a person like this genuinely desires to return to God and to enter the holiness of the Jewish People with a perfect heart, then every day and every hour he should think to himself literally: he was born today. He can strengthen his faith by binding himself to the holy Tsadikim. They are filled with the spirit of *Mashiach*, of whom it was

---

51. *Yebamot* 22a, *Bechorot* 47a

said, "I have today given birth to you." Forget the days and
years which may have passed. From *now on*, if one only lives
with this thought in mind at every moment, he will be worthy
of true closeness to God and healing will come for all the days
which passed. Everything will be transformed to good through
complete repentance.

   Moses said "You turn man to destruction and say: 'Return
ye children of men' " (Ps. 90:3). Our sages commented: You
turn man — to destruction" — the implication is, to the point
of destruction.[52] Even up to the time when life is destroyed,
still "You turn man" — and You receive his repentance. "You
say: 'Return ye children of men' " — return to the realm
beyond time. "For a thousand years in Your sight are but as
yesterday when it is past and as a watch in the night". (*Ibid.*
4). "Before the mountains were brought forth or ever You
formed the Earth and the world, even from everlasting to
everlasting, You are God" (*Ibid.* 2). Examine this Psalm
carefully and you will see that all of it deals with this realm
beyond time.   (Laws of Circumcision 4:17-19)

33.(78) Converts and *baalei teshuvah* — "masters of
repentance" — show the proper way to come close to God.
They acknowledge how far they are from God. At the same
time, they are confident that God Himself is very close to
them, because of His overwhelming love. This explains why
our sages said that when a person comes to convert he should
be asked, "What makes you think you are worthy of

converting?"[53] If he answers that he know himself and he is fully aware how unworthy he is, he acknowledges his own distance from God. He wants to draw near only through his trust in God's love — for God loves the proselyte. When a person like this comes along, our sages said that he should be accepted.

It is this line of thought that underlies the dialogue between Naomi and Ruth.[54] Naomi said, "There are four kinds of death penalty which the law courts are empowered to inflict." To this Ruth replies, "Wherever you die, there will I die" (Ruth 1:17). On the face of it it would seem that Naomi was trying to put Ruth off. Ruth possessed true modesty and had the most powerful yearning to convert. And here was Naomi suggesting that she might well commit a sin which would make her liable to the death penalty. What is the significance of Ruth's reply that she would die wherever Naomi died, i.e. subject to the same legal sanctions? The implication seems to be that she did not disagree that she might come to do something that would make her liable to the death penalty! Should she not have answered that she was confident of her purity and innocence and knew that she would never incur the death penalty? Actually, the exchange between Naomi and Ruth comes to teach us how those who are distant from God can draw near through their very consciousness of their distance. This is the meaning of the

53. *Yebamot* 47a, *Pesikta Zuta-Bo* 12:48
54. *Yebamot* 47b

words of the prophet: "Peace to those who are far and those who are near."(Is. 57:19)

Someone who thinks that he has already achieved closeness to God is necessarily far from the truth. This mistake has been the cause of all the disasters which have befallen the Jewish people. Never was Israel closer to our Father in Heaven than when the Holy Temple was standing. The Temple was the pinnacle of perfection, it was *the* place for all closeness to God. In the first Temple stood the Ark of the Covenent and the Tablets of Stone! Even so, those who had the privilege of standing in the holy Temple had to realize their own distance from God and from the holiness of this awesome place. Indeed the very root of their joy was their confidence that god brings even the most distant closer to Him. The very Temple itself — what was it? "Behold the Heavens and the Heaven of Heavens cannot contain Thee" (1 Kings 8:27). Still, God brought Himself down, he "contracted" Himself as it were, and caused His presence to dwell in the holy Temple. It was out of compassion alone that God gave the command that physical animals should be brought as offerings "for a sweet savour" (Ex. 29:41). But the people of the time made a mockery of all this. They thought that they had already achieved the ultimate good and that they had drawn close through their own endeavors. "Their hearts became high; therefore they have forgotten Me."(Hos. 13:6) This is what caused the destruction of the holy Temple.

What Naomi was saying to Ruth was that even though now her heart burned with a passion to draw close to holiness,

"Who knows — perhaps later on you might commit a crime and be sentenced to death." Ruth's only intention was that she should become perfectly righteous. Certainly not that she should . commit a crime. It was in the purity of her righteousness that she answered Naomi as she did. "I certainly have no confidence in my own righteousness. It may well be that I will fall, God forbid. But whatever happens — even if the Evil One brings me to whatever he brings me, — even if I should be deserving of death, still I accept upon myself all the obligations that the holiness of Israel carries with it. Wherever you die, there will I die.' " It was then that Naomi accepted her.

Ruth became truly righteous. From her seed, the Messiah will come and turn the whole world to good.

The same principle applies to everyone who wishes to draw close to the truth. He can do so only through knowing his distance. However close he becomes, he must always remember this distance. Not that it should be a reason for him to stay far away. The whole purpose is that this knowledge should help him draw close. "Peace to the one who is far and to the one who is near."[55] (Is. 57:19) (*Laws of Letting the Mother Bird Go.* 5:16, 17)

34.(83)   Our Rabbis said "You cn only strengthen those who are strong and you can only spur on those who are speedy".[56]

---

55. See Deut. 22:6,7
56. *Makot 23a, Bamidbar Rabbah 7:7*

In that case, where is the starting point?

In point of fact, in serving God there are many details which depend on one another and we simply don't know where the starting point is. But as far as we are concerned, the whole beginning, middle, end, and purpose of our life is to be found only in the Tsadik of Truth who is present in every generation.

The Tsadik of Truth is the Moses of the generation. Moses our teacher was the first teacher of all Israel. He is the fountain of all beginnings. With him are bound up our entire hope and purpose today. For in the words of King Solomon: "What was before will be again."(Eccl. 1:9)

Where the Tsadik himself — the Moses — starts from is something we cannot understand at all. It is not our part to be sceptical and to question how a man born of woman could rise to levels like this. So far as *we* are concerned, the start has been made for us. Moses went up to receive the Torah. Now we have it in our hands. And in every age we can draw upon its wisdom, through the guidance of the true Tsadikim.

From our earliest childhood we were brought up surrounded by the holiness of Israel. A boy is circumcised on the eighth day. He is trained in Torah and the divine commandments. With thanks to God we can draw tremendous inspiration from the plain fact that we were born as Jews. We have grown up surrounded by the holiness of Israel. We have faith in the Torah of Moses and in the words of all the Tsadikim who follow. We have faith that God's loving-kindness is unceasing regardless of what we may have gone through. The starting point is there. And because the foundation has already been laid the possibility exists that we too can be worthy of kindling the will to holiness.

The essence is desire — to long, yearn and pine for the Holy One, blessed be He. The very firmness of our will and desire itself gives us added strength. For the roots of all spiritual strength lie in *will.* Every person has free will, no matter what his circumstances. In any event, he should yearn and long to fulfill God's will and his commandments. This longing and yearning will themselves make him worthy of the true kindling of will. This is what is meant by the fear of God. It is easy to achieve because the will is always free. It only needs firmness and determination — to use all the force at your command. It is true that the one thing depends on the other. "You can only strengthen those who are strong." But the start has already been made through the strength and merit of the true Tsadikim.

See the beauty of Moses' call to Israel: "And now Israel, what does the Lord your God require of these, but to fear the Lord your God?" (Deut. 10:12) Our sages said, "For Moses, fear of God was a small thing."[57] What Moses meant was this, "After all my toil and labour on your behalf, (as explained in the preceeding chapters of Deuteronomy), I have attained a level of wisdom where fear of God is 'a small thing for me.' This wisdom which I can radiate to you, O Israel, provides you

---

57. *Berachot* 33b, *Tikuney Zohar* — foreward

with a firm base and a good starting point for your own endeavors. If you only strengthen yourself, you too, will achieve the kindling of the will and the true fear of God that are drawn from the burning fire of the wisdom of the true Tsadik."

We too can easily attain a level like this where fear of God becomes a small thing to us. For us the start has already been made by Moses and the true Tsadikim who followed him.

(Redemption of the Firstborn 5:33)

35.(84)   Even the complete sinner must have awe and fear of the greatness of God. He must fight with every ounce that is within him to rescue himself from his evil and draw himself up to a better way. He cannot excuse himself by saying that he has fallen so far that for him everything is permissible. Darkness and death will never be a hiding place for the workers of iniquity. Even in the lowest pit of hell you must fear God. All places are subject to His rule.   (Firstborn of Clean Beasts 4:14)

36.(86)   The *mussar* literature which deals with spiritual development contains many references to the seriousness of the various sins and the severe punishments which are associated with them. Many people are very frightened when they read all this. There are some who are so put off that they try to deny everything and become total atheists. But people like this have not understood the true intent of these passages. The root of the problem is that they have not understood the teachings of the Torah in the light of the guidance of the true

Tsadikim. They are convinced that they have sunk in their habits to the point where it is impossible to extricate themselves. The accounts of the punishments for the various sins, far from deterring these people, only make them conclude that they will never succeed in drawing close to God because the obstacles are too great. They abandon themselves completely to their old habits.

But God has pity on His people. Genuine fear of Heaven is an aspect of the messianic spirit. The true Tsadikim of every age have the power to radiate this spirit and the awe that goes with it even to people on the lowest levels. They too can be brought to a genuine awareness of God and to the knowledge that there is still hope for them because of God's abundant love.

People should not allow themselves to be deterred through the fear of punishment. On the contrary, it can actually bring them to great joy. If the "lower fear"[58] — the fear of punishment — does nothing more than stir people to follow the guidance of the true Tsadikim, it serves a good purpose. Their most basic rule is that you should seek out the good points within you. You can have joy from the simple knowledge that you come from the seed of Israel. Following this rule can bring even the worst person to wonderful joy. The heart of all the teachings of the Tsadikim is to live in joy. This is born out by the phrasing of Moses' warning to the Children

---

58. The lower fear is the fear of punishment, the higher fear of Heaven is the fear of God Himself, because of His greatness.

of Israel, where the whole intent is to arouse the fear of punishment. Why do punishments come? "Because you would not serve the Lord your God with joy and with gladness of heart." (Deut. 28:47)   (*Ibid.* 17:20)

37.(90) "God does not withold the reward of any creature"[59]. Not a single thing that a person does for the sake of Heaven is lost, regardless of whether it is large or small. Our sacred books may well say that when a wicked person does something good, it only adds to the force of the husks. But there is an inner meaning to these words which cannot be explained very well in a book. As a general rule, anyone who has pity on himself and tries to take himself in hand can achieve something by the good which he does. Even if it seems inadequate and tarnished in his own eyes, none of the good is ever lost.

The thing is to accustom yourself, little by little, to the ways of holiness. In the end you will surely be worthy of returning to God. There is no despairing. (Laws of Tithing 3:2)

38.(91) "All her persecutors overtook her in the narrow places" (Lam. 1:3) A person's desires and confusion can push him into such a narrow corner that there isn't room for him to turn to his right or his left. He may think that there is absolutely no hope for him at all. But if, under the full strength of all this pressure, he can force himself to cry out to

---

59. *Baba Kama* 38b, *Nazir* 23b, *Pesachim* 118a, *Horiyot* 10b

God — "I called upon the Lord from the narrow places" (Ps. 118:5) — then even if he turns himself no more than a hair's breadth toward God, this is precious indeed in the eyes of God. *Meitsar* — "the narrow places" — gets turned into *tsemer* — "wool,"[60] which is a reference to the strands of hair of the sacred Figure. The meaning of this is that the thirteen attributes of love are stirred and drawn down upon this man. They are the thirteen perfections of the sacred Figure, which is all love and pure goodness.

Through this it is possible to understand the significance of the ritual whereby, in Temple times, on the Day of Atonement, a thread of wool was tied to the scapegoat. The sins of all the year were whitened, as it is written "Though your sins be red like crimson, they shall be as wool" (Is. 1:18). The forgiveness which is granted on the Day of Atonement comes about because God finds even in the sinners of Israel any number of good threads. There are innumerable occasions when they also try to draw themselves from evil, even if only to the extent of one hair's breadth. This is still very precious in the eyes of God and it is this that brings about the revelation of the hairs of the sacred Figure. (Laws of the Offerings of Sheared Wool 3:2)

39.(93) There are many passages where we find God reproving and reprimanding the Children of Israel. At times there seem to be massive outpourings of abuse. But really the intention is always for the best. The purpose of all the abuse is

---

60. Meitsar — מצר : Tzemer — צמר

really to build up a case for the defense of Israel through which they can return to God.

There are times when Israel's behaviour reaches such a low point that even the small residue of goodness which still remains in them is covered by all the sins and failings. If God were to try to argue the case for a favorable verdict on account of this little bit of goodness, the prosecution would immediately rise up and find a thousand more reasons for condemning them, God forbid. But God loves mercy and he always longs for His people. So, in order to incline the scales towards mercy, God Himself, in His goodness and wisdom, steps forward and roundly abuses Israel with a torrent of contempt. He tells them they are just like all the other nations because of all the damage they have done. But as soon as He implies the comparison between Israel and all the other nations, the true goodness which is within Israel alone immediately becomes apparent. Earlier in the proceedings this goodness might have appeared to be worthless. And certainly when you consider the utter sublimity of the holiness of Israel at its roots, even the slightest hint of a transgression is really a terrible blemish. How much more so when their sins and transgressions are so serious that the little bit of good is scarcely recognizable at all! And even this scrap of good is sullied with all kinds of dubious motives and waste matter.

If God were to pay attention to the multitude of sins and transgressions, there could well be no hope left whatsoever. But God is "abundant in loving-kindness and truth." His desire is that the universe should stand, not that it should be destroyed. He knows the nature of our hearts and the prison which encloses us in this life. So in spite of everything, God Himself turns the tables in favour of Israel. He starts by comparing them to all the other peoples. "Are you not as the children of Kush to Me?"(Amos 9:7) Now, as soon as He starts making this comparison, everyone is forced to admit that "as far as the east is from the west" (Ps. 103:12), so is the gulf which exists between the worst Jew on the one hand and a heathen on the other. Compared to heathens, the people of Israel are filled with hundreds upon hundreds and thousands upon thousands of threads, strands and points of goodness. "Even the transgressors of Israel are as full of God's commandments as a pomegranate has seeds."[61]

It is precisely through God's scornful comparison of Israel to the heathens that all the merit and goodness within Israel is revealed. "And your people are all righteous" (Is. 60:21). Do they not don the *tallis* and *tefilin* every day? Do they not fast on the Day of Atonement? This explains why, as soon as the prophet says, "Are you not like the children of Kush unto me?" he immediately changes his tone "I will surely not destroy them. On that day I will erect the fallen tabernacle of David."(Ibid. 9:11) The comparison between Israel and the heathens throws into relief all the merits within Israel and through this the Messiah can come and restore the fallen tabernacle of David.

He is filled with abundant love and He has the power to

---

61.   Erubin 19a, Berachot 57a, Hagiga 27a, Sanhedrin 37a

uncover the merits of Israel, the threads and points of goodness that lie within them. Exactly the same line of reasoning underlies the words of Hosea. "Then said God: 'Call his name *Lo-ammi*, for you are not my people, and I will not be your God." (Hosea 1:9, 2:1). No sooner does the prophet announce this, than he says at once: "In the place where it was said unto them, 'You are not my people', there it shall be said unto them 'You are the sons of the living God.'"[62] (*Ibid.* 10)

40.(96) "And I have trusty witnesses, Uriah and Zechariah." On this the rabbis commented: "Uriah is a good omen for Zechariah!" Just as the prophecy of Uriah came true when the Temple was destroyed, so will the prophecy of Zechariah come true.[63] Zechariah prophesied that the redemption would come and the Temple would be rebuilt. This applies equally to the nation as a whole and to the redemption that will come to the soul of every single Jew. And when an individual mends his own way, this is the way that he personally rebuilds the holy Temple.

It is in man's nature to believe in the concept of "damage." People are aware that if their actions are at fault, they do great damage, destroying the holy Temple. But if this thought leads them to demoralization and despair, it is purely the work of the Evil One. If the possibility of damage exists, *so too does the possibility of repair!*[64] Behaviour can improve. Anything

---

62. See Pesachim 87a, b
63. Makot 24a
64. Lekutey Moharan B #112

that was damaged can be repaired. In the end we *will* be
worthy to return to God and the holy Temple will be rebuilt!
All the prophets and Tsadikim have assured us of this.
(*Witnesses* 11)

41.(97) The Torah is called "testimony" — as in the
expression, "The Two Tablets of Testimony." There had to be
two tablets, because the law requires two witnesses, one for
the highest point and one of the lowest point: Heaven and
Earth. For the testimony is that God's "kingship has power
over all", "in the Heavens above and over the Earth
below."(Deut. 4:39) As it is written: "If I ascend to the
Heavens, there You are, and if I make my bed in hell, behold
You are there." (Ps. 139:8)

These two Tablets of Testimony, the Torah, are faithful
witnesses. They remind and encourage everyone not to despair
of God's love. This is why the Tablets of Testimony were given
on the Day of atonement, the time of God's favour, a day of
forgiveness. It is the day when the path of return to God is
complete. The Torah comes to testify before Israel to the truth
of God's goodness and love. They extend to the two points, the
highest and the lowest. We must certainly be scrupulous
about keeping to the way of the Torah and avoiding the
slightest hint of sin and transgression. A person must strive all
the time to rise from one level to the next. "If I ascend to the
Heavens, there You are." God is there at the highest point. On
the other hand, we must also believe that regardless of the sins
and transgressions which we may have done and the damage
and destruction which they have caused to the entire world, it

is still within our own power to repair the damage. God is always with us. "If I make my bed in hell, behold You are there." God is there, too, at the lowest point. The hand of God is always stretched open to help us to retun and draw near through the path of repentance. The path is completed on the Day of Atonement, because the Dav of Atonement itself includes these two points, the highest and the lowest.

"The testimony of God is faithful, making wise the simple" (Psalms 19:7). The desire of the Torah is to bring wisdom even to the simple. The simple one is the person whose simplicity and gullibility have caused him to stumble through the spell of the evil inclination. The Torah calls this person and bears witness to him that if he returns, God will at once receive him in favour and accept his repentance. He will draw him near in His utmost love. Because of this, the simple person can also become wise. The only obstacle lies in the diffculty of believing that what was destroyed can still be repaired.[65] That is why King David had to cry out loud in this psalm: "The testimony of God is faithful!" The testimony is that God is the ruler of everything "in the Heavens above and on the Earth below." If you believe in the Torah's testimony about the gravity of sin and damage, you must also have faith in its testimony about the power it has to heal and repair. "Thy testimonies are very sure, O Lord, to the end of days" (Psalms 93:5). "To the end of days," because long and many are the days that we have been waiting, for the rebuilding of the holy Temple. This will be the culmination of our return to God. Then the healing will be

---

65. *Lekutey Moharan B,* 112

complete. As yet our salvation is not complete. Still we must be firm and have hope: Because "the testimonies of God are very sure."   (*Ibid*. 9, 10, 11, 12, 14)

42.(98) The evil inclination and its armies are the "false witnesses" which slip into the heart and say the opposite of all the above.

The Evil One is the tempter. Then he is the seducer. And finally he is the accuser.[66] First he tempts a person and leads him wherever he leads him. Then he comes in the role of accuser and casts his accusations in the worlds above and the worlds below. In the worlds above he works to alienate God from his people Israel, God forbid. Similarly, in the worlds below he works by making accusations in the hearts of men. He weakens people and demoralizes them with the idea that there is no hope left.

This is why King David cried out, "False witnesses rise up against me."(Ps. 27:12) It is also why God has given us two witnesses. On weekdays they are the sign of the Covenant and the *tefilin;* on the Sabbath they are the sign of the Covenant and Holy Sabbath itself.[67] These are the two true witnesses. They come to assure us that God's love is more powerful than anything. These two holy witnesses are the signs of that love. It is this which gives us the strength to crush and humble the false testimony of the evil inclination and his armies. (*Ibid.* 14)

---

66. *Baba Bathra* 16a
67. *Tekuney Zohar Hakdama*

43.(100) There are times when a man becomes "a fugitive
and a vagabond in the earth" (Genesis 4:14). He gets brushed
aside time and time again. It seems as if he is being totally
rejected. He struggles and struggles, searching, longing and
yearning for "Him whom my soul loveth" (Song of Songs 3:1).
Still it seems as if he will never be worthy of finding God. The
days and the years pass and the suffering continues. If only he
knew and believed that every single moment as he struggles
and searches, every single motion and gesture of writing and
pulling in yearning for the love of God and His holiness —
every single impulse in itself breaks down whole walls of iron
and gates of brass. Fresh obstacles may spring up immediately
after, but the struggle is not in vain. Not a single impulse for
holiness is ever lost. In the end he will be worthy of finding
God.

It is a part of man's condition that he must endure time
and change: seas, rivers, deeps, deserts and wildernesses filled
with serpents and scorpions. Only thus can he be worthy of
entering the gates of holiness. It is impossible to describe how
strong we must be. But there are people who think that what
was said does not apply to them because of the extreme trials
with which they are faced. They have become so entangled in
the nets and traps of despair that they think they will never be
worthy of returning to God. The Rebbe cried out against this,
"OY! NEVER GIVE UP HOPE!" The Yiddish words endure:
"Gevalt, zeit eich nit meyaesh!" The word gevalt he drew out
long.

Everybody can become worthy of drawing close to God
through following this one piece of advice: to search, seek, toil

and labour to return to Him. Then they will see the truth, that not a single impulse towards holiness is ever lost. (Laws of Collecting Debts from Orphans 3:17)

44.(111)   You cannot make love and kindness the only values in your life. If you try to do this, you will never achieve anything. You will end up following the impulses of your heart, all the while passively waiting for the love of God. This is not the way of the holy Torah.

On the other hand, you cannot allow strict justice nd reckoning to dominate your life. It would be impossible for the world to endure if God's attribute of strict justice were unmitigated by love, as our sages said. "You can see many people who have become distanced from God because of their own excessive judgment and reckoning."[68] They have been so strict with themselves and taken on so many burdens that they end up saying there is no hope for them because of their many sins and transgressions. Even if it is true that they transgressed, they must still rely upon God's love and mercy. Every hour of every day there is new hope, because God's love never ceases."

What is needed is a sense of balance. King Solomon was speaking about this when he said: "Do not be over-righteous and do not commit much evil."(Eccle. 7:16, 17) As our sages said, "If you've already committed some evil, don't commit any more."[69] Even somebody who has done an enormous

---

68. *Breishit Rabbah* 12:15
69. *Midrash Tehillim* 1:7, *Shabbos* 31b

amount of wrong should at least not do any more. The
smallest restraint which he puts upon his wrongdoings will be
for his own eternal good. In the end he will be worthy of
returning to God. There is no giving up in the world. God's
loving-kindness far outweighs the attribute of strict justice
which is the source of His punishments. With every sin or
transgression that a person does, God watches, concentrating
on every detail. "If a man hides in the hidden places, will I not
see him?"(Jer. 23:24) "From the place of His dwelling, He
looks." "He understands all their deeds".(Ps. 33:14, 15) If all
this is true of transgressions, it is much more true of good
thoughts and actions. Not a single good impulse is ever lost.

Now a person who tries to make unstinting love the only
principle of his life will inevitably come to break off the yoke
completely. Such a principle is the "husk of Ishmael."
Ishmael's father was Abraham, who was the epitome of
kindness and love. On the other side is the principle of
excessive reckoning and judgment. A person can make himself
fall through this, because of all the extra hardships which he
takes on himself. They make his service of God much too
difficult. Making strict justice the only principle comes from
the "husk of Esau". Esau's father was Issac, who was the
epitome of strict justice and reckoning. Esau invented totally
unnecessary laws: "How do we tithe hay and salt?" The extra
strictness which people take upon themselves can lead to great
damage.

Perfection comes when strict judgment and love are welded
into one. This concept is derived from Jacob, of whom it is
written: "Justice and kindness in Jacob."(Ps. 99:4) This is why

the couch of Jacob is called "perfect."[70]   (Gifts 5: 37, 38)

45.(112)   There is only the present — the instant you are standing at now. While this hour lasts don't think about the next.

46.(113)   No-one should ever despair of finding what he has lost. If only he is firm in his yearning, longing, and craving for God, there is hope that everything he has lost will be returned to him.

47.(116)   There are many people who were never brought up to learn Torah in any depth. They too have an obligation to study the Torah every day. Priority should always be given to the study of the legal codes.[71] At the very least, every day you should make sure that you study one law from one of the law codes, the *Shulchan Aruch*. You must also prick up your ears, listen and attend to the great and awesome voice of God which calls in the heart of every man, every day and at every moment, to bring him back to God. Even if you can do nothing else, you must long and yearn for God. This is most precious in His eyes.

The essence of everything is joy. Feel it in every bone of your body, when you bless and give thanks and praise to God for the unfathomable love He has shown us. He has chosen us from all the nations. He has given us the sweet treasure of His Torah, which is the source of all our life. These are the themes of the blessings which we say over the Torah. Everyone should

70. All his sons were true to God.
71. Yoreh Da'ah 246:4 *(Shach & Taz)*, *Mishne Berurah* 155:1#3, *Sichot Haran* 29

take great care with this. He should give praise and thanks to God even for the smallest crumbs of goodness which have come to him through the Torah.

The basic reason for the destruction of the Temple and exile of Israel was that the people of Israel did not take care to praise God for the Torah "Why was the land lost? Because they abandoned My Torah."[72] That means that they abandoned it completely, without seeing to it that in all circumstances they would snatch at least a bit of study time every day. "They did not listen to My voice."(Jer. 9:12) The meaning of that is that they did not prick up their ears and hear the voice of God which called in their hearts every day.

"They did not follow Me." Our sages explained that this means that they did not make the blessing over the Torah.[73] That is to say, they did not follow what is in fact a truly remarkable pathway to God, one that can save us from all the falls and backsliding in the world. Whatever happens to us, if we steel ourselves to bless God Almighty for the sweetness of our portion and our heritage, the sacred Torah, then regardless of who we may be, we can still find divine sparks and good points within us. Through them we can bring ourselves to joy and strength in God. If our forefathers had followed this path they would never have fallen into the depravities of the era of the First Temple. They would never have experienced the disasters which overtook them and the exile which they had to

---

72. *Nedarim* 81a
73. *Ibid.*

endure. All our hope today of returning to our land and seeing our sacred Temple rebuilt lies in our following this path.

(Loading & Unloading Beasts 4:35)

48.(117) There are certain secrets which have sufficient power to draw even those who are furthest away from God to return. These are the secrets which the greatest Tsadikim are wont to reveal in a whisper. Healing can come to the whole world when those who were far draw near to the service of God. If you want to understand the reason for this veil of secrecy and whispering, it is the same as the reason why, after the *Shema*, we whisper the words "Blessed be the name of his glorious kingdom for ever and ever."[74] Understand this well. "The mystery of God is shared with those that fear Him."(Ps. 25:14) If you believe in this mystery, there is hope in escaping "the trap that they have laid for me." "My eye is always to the Lord, for he draws me out of the trap around my feet."(Ps. 25:15) (Laws of Abandoned Property and the Property of the Proselyte 4:22)

49.(118) The spiritual enlightenment which we receive during the period of Passover and the Counting of the Omer comes out of sequence. This is explained in the literature that deals with the inner meaning of our religious practices. At this time of the year, instead of the lesser illuminations coming first and leading to greater illuminations, things happen the opposite way. There are tremendous differences in the light which comes down on each of the days of this period. The

---

74. *Pesachim* 56a

reason why the illumination has to come out of sequence is because of the hold of the forces of the "Other Side." We are still in the grip of the uncleanness of Egypt and it is only if the illumination is out of sequence that we are able to receive it. Now, for the people of Israel as a whole, spiritual illumination only comes in this unusual way during this particular period. But so far as the individual is concerned, as long as he is not yet cleansed of his sins, he is still engaged in his personal exodus from Egypt. For such a person even at other times of the year, illumination can still only come out of sequence because of the continued hold over him of his Egypt — the uncleanness of his own sins.

The one goal of all wisdom, knowledge and intelligence is to know and acknowledge God Almighty, and to draw close to Him. Every single day has within it a unique wisdom. This is the essence of the goodness of that day; it is the light of the sun which shines that day. Each day also has its own barriers. Not everyone is able to rise to the goodness of the day because the light is covered by darkness. This is explained in the holy Zohar. This darkness is the husk which you encounter before you come to the fruit. It is the sum total of all the problems, difficulties, accidents etc. which crop up in the life of every person every day. Fresh distractions bind him all the time, to the point that he wants to write off that day. "Today I won't be able to serve God. I'll put it off till tomorrow." So it continues from day to day.

You must totally reject this mentality. You have to make the breakthrough *today* — to break down the barriers and obstacles and to draw out the unique goodness which exists only *today*. You must draw down the illumination and the wisdom which are exclusive to *this* day. It is the power of the illumination that is possible on a given day, which determines the strength of the barriers and the obstacles that crop up on that day to cover the goodness. Just as there are differences in the visions and perceptions of God which are possible on particular days, so there are distinctions among the barriers and the obstacles which hold them in check. That is why a person should never lose heart when he sees that he was previously able to pray with a certain degree of devotion, and he had a certain respite from all the distractions and confusions in his mind. Suddenly he finds that they are all back with even greater force than before. The reason could be that on the previous occasions, one of the greater illuminations was being radiated to him. The strength of the enlightenment that comes because of them far outweighs any barriers which the forces of the "Other Side" can erect. But now he has to receive a different degree of illumination. It could be one of the lesser illuminations, or even one on the level of the "smallest of the small" illuminations. Over these, the forces of the "Other Side" have tremendous hold. That is why he finds it so hard to stand up to all the obstacles and barriers which confront him now. But he must still have faith that there is a unique goodness present today as well. Therefore, he has no option but to smash the barriers.

The barriers correspond exactly to the particular good which is present only today. The strength which you need every day must be appropriate to the demands of that particular day. There are times when it may be absolutely impossible for you to pray in the appropriate way. You still must not lose sight of the fact that today is also a day! Today will be counted among the days of your life. If in the end it is totally impossible for you to pray in the correct way, at least you must make every effort to do something else. Try to speak to God in your own words. Or recite some of the prayers which are not part of the regular service. Try to say *them* with sincerity. Or else you can try to learn something extra. Or make an effort to do something kind for somebody else.

"It was God's desire that Israel should acquire merit, that is why He gave them a copious Torah and many commandments." With thanks to God there is plenty of food for us every day. There is plenty of variety in the different areas of the Torah that we can study. There are all kinds of commandments for us to carry out.

Exert yourself to the full and never make the mistake of writing off today. You should think to yourself that you only have this single day. "Today, if you will listen to His voice."(Ps. 95:7)   (Laws of Deposits 4, 5-8)

50.(124)   The essence of the holiness of Israel lies in the commandments of *tzitzis* and *tefilin*. Through them we draw the light of truth into the world. They are a "lamb" and an "ox." There are times when the forces of the "Other Side" become so strong that they succeed in stealing the lamb and the ox.[75] They can even slaughter them or sell them. This is

---

75. See Exodus 21:37

what happens when a person falls to such a level that he stops wearing *tzitzis* and laying *tefilin*. He has lost the very root of his holiness. But he should never give up his lamb and his ox for lost. He must force himself to search for them — to seek to return to God in truth. Otherwise what will become of him? In the end he too will have to search for his eternal goal. God will certainly help him to find the thief. If he finds the thief with the sheep and the ox in his hands he will get back double. And if the thief slaughtered them or sold them, the victim will get back four-fold and five-fold.   (Theft 5:15)

51.(126) "When King David went out to battle, he made himself hard as wood. But when he was sitting and studying the Torah, he made himself as pliant as a worm."[76]

When you wish to draw near the holy, you must bring a hard stick with you. This hard stick is the stength and merit of all the good points you have, and especially the strength and merit of the true Tsadikim who give you protection. But you should only bring this stick to use against the Evil One. His aim is to confuse you and steal from you even the small amount of devotion which you were attempting. He tries to demoralize you by pointing to all your flaws. You must humble him by pointing to your good points.

But none of this will help you when you come before the Almighty himself. There you must stand like an impoverished beggar and pour out your heart like water. You must beg and

---

76. *Moed Kattan* 16b

entreat God. You must not try to depend on any merit whatsoever. Nor should you try to force the hour. You must make yourself pliant as a worm.

52.(127) You must never try to force the hour, even when you wish to draw yourself closer to holiness. You must wait patiently. You must simply hope that God will send His salvation. You must wait until you are worthy of expressing yourself before God with love, begging and entreating. Wait — and in the end you will receive words which burn like coals of fire. And then you must wait some more. You must be patient and wait for your request to be fulfilled, so that you can draw close to God and achieve your fulfillment. And even while you are waiting, be sure not to let yourself be distracted from your good. You must never forget the longing and yearning which you must have for God.

53.(128) A thread of hair is a precious thing. All your life you hang by only a single hair. It only takes one hair's breadth for a man to come to ruin. And with a hair's breadth you can repair everything.

A hair's breadth in holiness is precious indeed. God, in His love, gave us numerous commandments which have to be carried out every day. Every single Israelite can draw himself from evil to good by doing as much as he is able to. Each morning, he leaves everything and goes out of the house in order to go to the synagogue. He puts on his *tallis* and *tefilin*. He says his prayers. In all these things there are countless good sparks. These are the "threads of holiness" which are precious in God's eyes.

Next come the temptations and desires which assail us every day. Even a hair's breadth gesture to resist them is precious in God's eyes. "He knows our nature," He knows the strength of the evil urge which is planted in every individual. That is why every gesture which a person makes to escape it is precious in God's eyes. Man's lot is to be placed in this physical world, which is filled with the husks which tangle their way around everybody. A person must use sense in his life. He must guard himself against even the slightest hint of a thought which is beyond the bounds of holinees. If you go off course by a hair's breadth, you can end up in a complete wilderness. Everybody knows that all his problems began through a mere hair's breadth. But a hair's breadth can also be the start of the ascent. You may have fallen far. But every single hair's breadth that you draw yourself up from the evil is precious in God's eyes beyond all measure. In the end all the threads will be gathered together. Then you will be worthy of a true perception of Godliness. All the "contractions" through which God makes himself known are threads of hair. Even the greatest Tsadikim were hanging only by one thread of hair. (Laws of Damages 4:3)

54.(130)   Life must be a continuous progression from level to level. It is an inevitable part of this progress that before any rise there must always be a fall. This is a moment of great danger. It takes a fierce battle to tear off the thick curtain of darkness which comes before the light. Fighting this battle is a task the Tsadikim are engaged in every day. The same is true for all people who want to lead an honest, true life. There is no-one in the whole creation who does not have to endure this trial of darkness before the light. Even someone on the lowest level has to endure countless rises and falls as soon as he stirs himself even slightly in the direction of holiness. This applies to somebody who is literally inside the earth, even in the lowest pit of hell. Once he is stirred to draw himself up, there will be level after level. In the physical world this is perfectly obvious. You have the ground floor, the first floor, the next floor up, and so on. Now you can begin to see how many levels there are from earth up to Heaven. And so on, from Heaven further upwards. The same is true in the depths of the earth. How many pits and channels and fissures there are! To get out of them you must climb from one level to the next. Even if the level you have to climb to is still in the very depths of the earth, you will have to encounter obstacles before you can break through to it. There are tremendous battles and obstacles to be encountered every time you want to do something holy. At times you simply don't win. You slip and you fail in the test. When this happens, you must start all over again. That is why you need such great strength and single-mindedness. At all times you must concentrate on the goal. Whoever you are and wherever you are, you are duty-bound to fight the war of God with all your might. The very effort which you put into the struggle to climb up is precious in God's eyes. If you labour, toil and pray all day that God should release you from the places you have fallen to, in the end you will certainly find true good. The lowest falls will be transformed into the greatest ascents.   (Parapet & Physical Safety 2:5)

55.(133)   The light of the infinite which God has revealed is hidden within "contractions" through the divine attribute of stern justice. But the sternness can be sweetened by wisdom. Each single "contraction" has a unique wisdom which sweetens it alone. But there is also the Comprehensive Wisdom. This is the Supernal Wisdom, through which "contractions" and stern judgments are sweetened. But it is only possible to draw from this wisdom through the numerous books which contain the teachings of the Torah.

Wisdom is Man. "Contraction" is Woman. The union of man and woman, wisdom and "contraction," comes about through a "book" the marriage contract, or the document of betrothal. Their separation also comes about through a "book" — the divorce document. All union and separation can come about only when we rise to the level of Supernal Wisdom and draw from it by means of a book.

Sometimes there are arguments and quarrels between a man and his wife. They come before the Rabbi in order to arrange the divorce document. This is usually precisely the moment for a reconciliation. the love and bond between them can become even stronger. The reason for this is that they receive an illumination from this sweet Supernal Wisdom. On the plane of this Wisdom all the harsh judgments and disputes in the entire creation are sweetened. If the couple does divorce, it is only because they did not have the strength to receive the full sweetness of this wisdom. Because of this they were not able to sweeten the dispute between them. All that they could manage was to rise to this level in order to annul their bond and union at their highest source. This is what happens in divorce.

God is filled with compassion. Long ago He chose us from all the peoples when we were assembled at Mount Sinai. This was "the day of His marriage" (Song of Songs 3:11). The marriage came about when God gave us the "book" of the Torah and swore to our forefathers and to us that He would never ever divorce us. Even if we find, time and again, that God uses expressions of rejection and separation from His people, as it were, His true intention is only to draw us closer.

Our sages compared this to the case of the king who was angry with his wife.[77] He sent for the scribe to write out the bill of divorce. In the time it took to prepare it, the king was reconciled to his wife. He said to the scribe "Go and write her a second marriage contract."

The meaning of this is to be found in the explanation alone. It would only be possible to annul the long-standing bond between the two of them by ascending to the level of Supernal wisdom. But God is filled with compassion. As soon as the ascent is made, His love is aroused and the divorce proceedings are turned on their head. Not only is the bond not annulled, but on the contrary, an awesome illumination comes down to smash all the "contractions" and stern judgments that exist in all of creation. All the anger and fury which God ever had against the people of Israel, whether as a whole or against any single individual within it — everything is sweetened and annulled through this comprehensive Supernal Wisdom. The disputes, the rejections and the separation only caused the matter to be brought to this level. Now the entire situation is

---

77. *Rashi Hoshea* 2:1, Sifri

turned on its head and only sweetness is drawn down. "Go and write her a second marriage contract."

The purpose of all the rejections we receive from God is only to draw us closer. God's only intention in summoning the scribe to write the bill of divorcement is to bring about the true good. "In the place where it was said unto them 'You are not my people,' there it shall be said unto them 'You are the sons of the living God' " (Hosea 1:10). "In the place" — in the very place where the separation is felt most strongly and with the greatest anguish, precisely there everything will be turned on its head, and be sweetened. In the end, "It shall be said unto them 'You are the sons of the living God.' " This place is the source of all the sweetness in the creation. (Laws of Divorce 3:4)

Rabbi Nachman was once asked: "If the Messianic redemption did not come in previous generations, with Tsadikim on the level of *Moshe Rabbenu*, Rabbi *Shimon* bar *Yochai*, the *Ari Hakadosh*, and the *Baal Shem Tov*, how can it come now, when the generations are on a much lower level?" Rabbi Nachman answered with a parable.

Once there was a great city surrounded by extraordinarily strong fortifications. All the powers in the world had plans to capture it. The various kings threw in their strongest forces, but they were wiped out. Then a certain wise king came along. He examined the walls carefully and reckoned that if he were to take *all his forces* and hurl them against the fortifications he could capture the city. He did so, but *all his forces* were wiped out. Upon examining the walls however, he realized that they were on the verge of collapse even though from the outside they appeared firm. The king realized that now, even with the elderly, the sick and even the children he could take the city. He gathered them together and they succeeded. *They* destroyed the wall and took the city.

So it will be with the redemption. The great Tsadikim of the past all fired their arrows against the forces of the "Other Side" and the Angel of Death. Their foundations, though they appear as strong as before, are totally shaken. Anyone in our era can come along and finish off the forces of the "Other Side" and bring about the redemption and the coming of the Messiah. (Ma'asiot Umeshalim page 37)

THE TZADIK WHO FELL INTO A DEPRESSION

It is well known what a negative state of mind depression is. It is important to keep well away from it. One should try to live one's life with vigour and draw oneself upwards. When a person starts serving God, every single movement and advance that he makes is extraordinarily precious in God's eyes, even if he moves no more than a hair's breadth. Man's condition is to live in the physical body in the material World of Action, the lowest of the four worlds. This makes every movement and advance difficult for him. That is why each one is precious in God's eyes.

There is a story of a certain Tzadik who fell into a terrible state of depression and heaviness. When depression and heaviness attack a Tzadik it is especially difficult for him because they attack with extra force. In the end this Tzadik fell into such a state of lethargy and apathy that he literally could not move from his place. He wanted to cheer himself up and make himself happy and pull himself out of the depression. But there was nothing he could find to cheer himself up about and climb out of it. Every time he found some reason to be happy there was an insidious voice inside him which pointed to some aspect of that thing to be depressed about.

Then he started to cheer himself up with the thought — as we say in the daily prayers — that God "did not make me a heathen". This really *is* something to be happy about, and here there is no limit to the joy we should feel. It is impossible to conceive of the unbridgeable gulf, the innumerable differences which exist between the holiness to be found in even the least

significant Jew and the total uncleanness and impurity of the
heathen. When a person reflects on the love God has shown
him by not making him a heathen, without question he will
come to a state of joy. And this joy is one that can never be
mingled with depression. When a person tries to cheer himself
up with the thought of something he did or achieved himself,
there is always room for an admixture of depression. Any
number of deficiencies might have crept in. Such things make it
impossible for the person to feel happy without reservation and
be able to draw himself up to a higher plane. But the fact that
"He did not make me a heathen" is something which God alone
has given. It was through God's love and mercy that He did not
make the Jew a heathen. Since it is a gift of God it is impossible
for there to be any fault in it. Therefore the joy it brings must
be perfect. No matter what state a Jew might be in, there is still
no limit to the distance that separates him from the heathen.

So the Tzadik we were speaking about started to cheer
himself up with this thought. Little by little he pulled himself
higher and felt happier. Moment by moment he became more
and more joyous... until he attained the same joy that Moshe
Rabbenu attained when he ascended to receive the tablets of
stone. With the joy and elevation that the Tzadik achieved his
soul flew thousands upon thousands of miles in the upper
worlds — light years! He took a look at himself and saw how
far he was from the place where he had been at the beginning.
But this actually made him quite worried, because he thought
he would fall to some other place and then everyone would
notice and be surprised that he had disappeared all of a sudden,
whereas a Tzadik always wants to live modestly without

attracting attention. His joy began to wane — because there is always a measure to joy. It comes and it goes. When joy begins to wane it does so gradually, ebbing little by little.

When the Tzadik began to descend from the place he had risen to at the climax of his joy, he did not retrack and start returning to the place he had started from along the path of his flight in the Upper Worlds. In actual fact he simply dropped down to the point he had ascended from... Amazingly, after he dropped down he found that he was actually back in the place he had originally started off from. When the Tzadik took a look at where he was, it seemed that he was in exactly the same place where he had been at the outset. He had not moved from there at all... except, perhaps, by a single hair's breadth, an infinitesimally small distance which the human mind cannot even conceive of; only God can conceive of such a distance.

The Tzadik simply could not get over the fact that in the Upper Worlds he had flown so far, yet in the lower worlds he had not advanced at all. It proved to him how precious in God's eyes is even the smallest forward movement that a man makes in this world, even if it is no greater than a single hair's breadth. Compared with this, distances of thousands and thousands of miles are of no account.

Let us try to understand this. The fact is that this material world is merely the central point in the middle of all the spheres which make up the universe. (All this is explained in the writings of the kabbalists.) When one considers the upper worlds, world upon world, it is clear that our planet Earth is no more than a mere dot.

Now it is obvious that if you draw a number of straight lines emerging out of a central dot, near the dot all the lines are close together. But the further one gets from the dot, the greater the distance between the various lines. If the length of the lines is very great the distance between them becomes enormous, in spite of the fact that at the bottom, near the dot, they are very close together. This can be seen in the illustration.

Imagine lines stretching out from our lowly Earth and reaching the spheres which rotate about the Earth. From what we have said it follows that even if on earth one moves only a hair's breadth, in the place of the spheres the point above one's head has moved thousands of miles from the place where it was 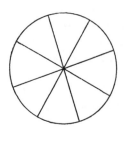 at first. Consider the massive distances in the realms of the spheres, where there are innumerable stars, each one of them the size of our entire universe. Now imagine these lines from Earth extending even further to the regions beyond the highest of the spheres, to the Upper Worlds — worlds whose immensity makes even the spheres pale into insignificance. One can see that the motion caused by even this hair's breadth movement on earth from one point to the next has now become infinite in its extent. Here on earth the motion may have been no more than the merest hair's breadth, and the person who made it is under the impression that he has not moved at all. (For the actual distance is inconceivable to all except God.) Even so, in the Upper Worlds the distance moved can be worlds